PRAISE FOR **THE ABUNDANT YOGI**

"Ari is awesome!!

Leadership, drive, and passion are the traits Ari not only exhibits in her life and business but also instills in her teams and community.

Leadership is not only about doing the things right...it's about doing the right things.

Keep your eye on this powerful soul. She will take your game to another level!"

— Jim Bunch, Business Coach and International Speaker

"The moment I knew I needed focus and clarity of where to take my time, energy and business, I worked with Arianne and took her courses and it helped me tremendously in taking the right decisions on my offerings and value. Just 4 short months later I saw a huge different in my revenues, exactly 3x more from what I was making. It was the push of clarity and empathy I needed to recognize my dharma and achieve my goals. Highly recommend her expertise!"

— Laura Velazquez, Creator of LEVA Massage

"Ari's experience and direction have been invaluable to me as a small business owner. She encourages me to think outside of my mental box and reach for the stars!"

— Victoria Arvizu, Founder of High Energy Fusion Yoga

"I can not describe how grateful I am with Arianne. Since I started working with her I found many ways to be more effective with my time, deliberate with my mission and organized in my work! I admire her so much. She taught me how about be more clear communicating, value myself and business. Still learning with every session we have!"

— Paola Villegas, Founder of Blissful Yoga Miami

Big thanks to my hubby Marcel and my baby girl Solenne!

THE
ABUNDANT
YOGI

GROW YOUR YOGA BUSINESS
WITHOUT LOSING YOUR SOUL

Thank you Sandy !
to all the abundance,
♡, arianne

ARIANNE "OM" TRAVERSO

ISBN: 978-0-9898638-3-4

Written and illustrated by Arianne "OM" Traverso

Printed in the United States of America

www.bizyogi.co/abundant

Knowing we can serve as
healers, givers, and game changers
is my legacy
to you and to the world.

Contents

1

Laying The Foundation

Get On Your Business Yoga Mat

Tears of frustration rolled down my face. I sat behind the computer, attempting to reconcile six weeks' worth of transactions in QuickBooks, including over 750 transactions, purchases, and returns, and payroll records for over 20 teachers. I was tearing my hair out because the numbers would not match. I could hear my mother's voice in my head—"Your numbers must match to the cent"—but no matter what I did, they just weren't adding up.

I wanted to throw my laptop across the room.

It was 11 pm. I had been working frantically all night and hadn't even had dinner. My dog was looking at me, pissed off because we hadn't gone on our regular walk. Oh, and I had to teach the next day's 7 am class because the teacher had cancelled last minute and no one else could sub. Plus, the graphics for the workshop weren't done, we needed to get the Facebook event out and send the newsletter. Despite my meltdown, I continued to work until after midnight to get everything done.

I was burning the candle at both ends and not practicing as often. Every time I was in the studio, I was too concerned about the hairball on the floor or the front desk not selling the package we needed to sell because the A/C duct had been stolen the night before and our landlord had raised our rent. UGH.

After the first six months of owning my yoga studio, I had a revelation: this business shit is real. Owning a yoga studio requires a different set of skills than being an independent freelancing yogini. I was missing skills that I had never been taught, systems that I never created, and a team to support me. I was not an accountant, manager, or anything else but a great yoga teacher with a background in graphic design and marketing.

Enough was enough. I decided to take business into my own hands. I hired my first business coach, who opened up my mind to possibilities, taught me structure and the fundamentals I was missing. This led to more crying during the "Oh shit!" moments, but led to new insights and helped me own my life and business again.

○ ○ ○

Why I Wrote This Book

The title says it all: *The Abundant Yogi*. I'm fascinated with the words *creation* and *expansion*, because they connect me to what yoga did for me and what it's doing for others around the world. Yoga is how I lead my life daily and why decided to dedicate my time to helping others do the same thing. Biz Yogi is the place where we all level each other up as leaders, manifesting superstars—creators of programs that heal and radically change the world one om...one touch...one asana at a time.

I've been blessed to learn from some of the top coaches and leaders in the world on how to run a successful business. Know that the underlying magic starts with your WHY. In this book, I delve deep into this underlying passion to work on your business and work on yourself so that you change from the inside and shine. It's your chance to step in and shine, to create and radiate and make your lifestyle a reflection of your soul—shiny and happy!

For the past five years, I've helped yogis and healers, business-minded and yogi-hearted souls just like you create programs they never thought they would, make more money with smarter work, and turn their passions into a profitable and sustainably abundant business and life.

Without the right knowledge (buddhi) and strategy, owning a yoga studio can be an enormous challenge. The roles of business owner and yogi do not always go well together in our belief structure. As a teacher, you are focused on helping your students experience yoga in its purest form with your unique style of delivery, rather than the strategies required to run a successful business.

Perhaps you ditched your old career to become an instructor because you were tired of the day-to-day and wanted something more meaningful. This might mean you have a business, marketing, accounting, or law degree—which can be helpful when operating a real money-making business.

Being a great teacher does not mean you are a great businessperson. But in this book, I lay it out for you so you can avoid my mistakes and keep your sanity.

I embarked on this business journey as a result of my "Oh shit!" moment, along with an internal desire to see expansion and growth in the world, with yogis at the helm as inspirational leaders.

You have a vision of your ideal life, but you don't know how to get from where you are now to your dream. You're reading this book because you know something needs to change. Your reason might look different from mine, but you know that you want to make an impact.

As yoga instructors and guides, our quest toward the center of our souls has led us down the path of opening studios, often teaching 20 to 30 classes a week and selling goods and services, all in the quest of being free, yet we are stuck on a hamster wheel.

How can we create a thriving yoga business and stay true to the principles of yoga? In this path toward union, self-realization, and spreading light and love, yogis and yoginis alike have turned the yoga world upside-down and the business downside up.

Go back to India some five thousand years ago and you see a very different image, don't you? One without hot yoga, lululemon, or power vinyasa. It looks more like a few yogis in loincloths sitting in nature, just being and practicing.

So how did our beloved yoga turn into a commercialized version of sadhus and gurus in spandex? How can we focus on feeling aware, abundant, and amazing in the yoga business without losing our souls or sanity?

Yoga is about awareness. I envision yogi-preneurs stepping into a place where you are fully aware of business, creating amazing programs and transformations for your students. As a result, they are stepping into financial abundance so that the impact resonates worldwide larger and faster.

Yogis make decisions that affect the world on a larger scale. You step into leadership and use your power to help others in a more impactful way. I know that my coaching and programs have the potential to affect millions. You are an integral part of this piece. There's also a connection between what yoga means to you as a way of life and becoming successful and abundant as a yoga business. From the depth of my heart, I visualize you yogi-preneurs making the money you want and giving back in a much more meaningful way.

The business of yoga is a modern concept, which stems from two instances. First, there are a lot of opportunities out there. The world is moving toward a holistic lifestyle, and the trend is not stopping. There are so many ways to systematize, create, and enjoy how you've chosen to make money that help others and yourself. Second, you want a lifestyle consistent with your values and beliefs as a yogi, which means setting up a business in a way that prevents overwhelm and burnout and enjoying everything you are doing.

Who Should Read This Book?

You are a yogi-preneur who has a bigger vision for your life and wants to make a ripple effect throughout the world. If you've ever wanted to reach more people, to step into your business as an owner who works *on* your business versus just *in* your business, then you're in the right place. Yogis who have drive, ambition, and the desire to be successful can make such amazing strides with guidance.

You should read this book if you feel like you've been teaching yoga for so long and you're tired of living paycheck to paycheck. You know you are not stepping into your fullest potential because you simply don't know how.

My goal is for you to know that going into your studio or class every day can provide the lifestyle you deserve, and allow you to help others on a larger scale than you ever dreamt possible.

As you read, you will have the opportunity to clarify why you do what you do. You will reflect on what you're doing and how it is getting done. You will learn how to sustain yourself in abundance and to create a mindset and emotional space so you are an empowered and fulfilled yogi. You'll gain a different perspective on business and how to marry it with a yoga practice. When your cup is full, you can then give from that abundant space.

This book has two parts: Part 1 is for the yoga pro who makes a living from teaching, leading retreats, trainings, and wants to contribute your knowledge to a captive audience; Part 2 is for those who own a yoga studio that needs some extra love or plan to open one. Use it as a how-to manual: check things off as you go, noting what you have in place and what you're missing.

I am here to support you, so please feel free to connect with me.

Owning A Yoga Business

Let's start with something that several of my mentors and coaches have done for me: getting crystal clear on a vision. This is what keeps you going and moving forward whether times are great or not so great. Vision is what keeps you steadfast in creating your ideal life.

Are you ready to be part of this entrepreneurial journey?

What does it mean to own a yoga business? It's anything related to the practice and lifestyle of yoga that brings you income. A business is something you do that gives you money in exchange; a hobby is something you do for fun. Business can be full-time or part-time. You can put in all your energy or some of it and know that what you put in is what you get out of it.

Take a few moments and visualize your ideal future without creating limits on the possibilities. Stay strong in your authentic desire for your life. One of my coaches Jim Bunch said to me, "Remember where you were five years ago and where you are now. Do you think if you'd had a vision and plan you would've arrived here faster?"

Throughout the book, including one just a few paragraphs below, you will find sections labeled Put It Into Practice. These activities are designed to allow for immediate application of what you've learned so you can maximize the advice for your own yogi practice and business.

In yoga, there are four basic principles, also known as the four aims, called the Purusharthas.

- Artha: prosperity, economic values

- Dharma: righteousness, moral values

- Kama: pleasure, psychological values

- Moksha: liberation, spiritual values

    The Purusharthas are the blueprint for human fulfillment. Working with them helps you create a satisfyingly balanced, meaningful life at the deepest and most holistic level. They offer a way for evaluating your life and making good decisions. Knowing your goals brings meaning to your spiritual practice. — Deepak Chopra

Because you get so enthralled in life's daily duties, you sometimes get stuck in a "this is it" mind state without going a little bit further to see what these can bring.

You may be saying, "Ari, I am a yogi—I live in the present!" I get it, but it's okay to cast your vision into the future too.

put it into practice

Consider what you would like to accomplish related to each of these four principles.

Write down your vision for the future.

In 1 year, I will...

_____

_____

In 5 years, I will...

_____

_____

In 10 years, I will...

_____

_____

Now that you have a vision in mind and because this book is about abundance, we'll dive deeper into Artha. The purpose of this is to have enough assets to live on and care for your family without being greedy. Ask yourself, "What do I see as being truly valuable?"

Here are some suggestions.

- Don't chase money. Create a way to attract it to you.

- Work based on your natural abilities and strengths.

- Love what you do fully.

- Trust in the infinite organizing power of the Universe.

- Are you managing your life and business based on these four tenets?

If you are already a yogi entrepreneur (or yogi-preneur as I like to call it) or you've decided you want to be one, know that it can create so many opportunities for you to step up to the plate in a more significant way and to help more people. Know that your business can be a very important launching pad, and it can also be the rest of your life. And nothing is wrong or right about that—it's just understanding what you desire, staying constantly connected to those desires, and knowing you are the creator of your own life.

I did an exercise once where I wrote 100 goals in 1,000 days. Little did I know it was part of my ideal life. In that list, one of my life goals was "Open a studio." I didn't really believe I would actually do everything I wrote on there, but I completed about 80 of them! Some took me longer and I got help with many. But know that if you dream it and take action, it's 100% doable.

Having a vision has expanded my life in a way I never would have imagined. Being a yoga studio owner, a leader, and yoga conference organizer were my biggest gifts, because they opened me up to learning about business and falling in love with it so much that I'm now able to help hundreds of people do the same. I've grown through the consulting work I do, because it was a platform for me and created such a beautiful community of people who are still in my life.

Even in the moments of frustration, those "Oh shit!" moments are when the "Oh yeah" comes. So have a stronger vision and cast it toward the future.

Constantly check in to ask yourself...

- Why do I want to achieve this goal?
- What do I want to create and bring into my life?
- How am I operating within my life? Is it with joy, ease, and breath? Is it fun?
- Am I still me, or did I lose myself or sacrifice moments of my life for a business?

Just being honest with yourself about these things will be key.

What It Means To Be The Teacher

You are a teacher—an instructor and a bringer of light. You love what you do because of the change you see in your students. Every time you teach a class, the light in their eyes and the change in their state fuels you.

You also have very personal reasons you chose this path, and this is your big WHY. This is your center and why you're reading this book. The WHY is the core of everything you do. Check out the video by Simon Sinek, "The Power Of Why." It's spot on about all this.

Ask yourself...

- Why did I choose this path?
- What does it mean to be a professional yogi?
- Who do I serve?
- What is my mission and my legacy?

This journey, whichever way it takes you—whether it is opening a studio, being a freelance yogi pro, or moving into a different way of sharing your knowledge—all starts with a few basic pieces such as your...

- Brand

- Commitment

- Message

- Money

- Niche

- Vision

I'm going to give you some business models that can generate revenue really quickly. For me, knowing this was a game-changer in terms of options that resonated with my soul and strengths. You want to hash this out in the very beginning.

As I mentioned, not only did I have a professional yoga career for a long time, I also owned a studio. But it wasn't the right kind of business for me, which was a blessing in disguise.

Here's a list of different business styles that might suit you according to your personality, strengths, and lifestyle choices. Note that not all of these might apply to you. They are divided into two categories where you trade time for money and where you can create more leverage.

Your Time

- **Classes** are your source of connection to people who could potentially turn into loyal customers.

- **One-on-one clients** are where you get premium prices for your time. It's a limited model but can be billed at a higher rate.

- **Retreats** are one of my favorite models. They require your time but are also scalable. When done correctly, holding a retreat can change lives and provide solid revenue.

- **Trainings** are another hybrid model and a great way to showcase your knowledge. Thes and retreats are considered higher-ticket items.

- **Workshops** are a perfect offering between a class and a brief training. It's a group model and provides value for the attendees.

Leveraged

- **Educational material** showcases your expertise as well as your passion.

- **Live events** create a sense of community and provide a larger platform for yourself and others.

- **Licensing** products and services is a great way to make passive revenue.

- With **network marketing** or direct sales, you sell a product, which helps you build leadership and can be very lucrative in the long run.

- **Online programs** are a great way to teach and connect with people.

- You can create and sell **physical products** like apparel or accessories from your studio.

- A brick-and-mortar **studio** can operate without you if the systems are set up correctly.

I've often seen yogis follow a path that looks like this:

Classes → Workshops → Retreats or Classes → Workshops → Studio

This is a solid model but don't limit yourself to this flow, as there are many options.

Part 1 of this book is relevant to a yogi-preneur lifestyle. In Part 2, we'll dive deeper into what owning a studio feels and looks like.

The Riches Are
In The Niches

What is a niche? It's your corner of the market, your specialty, where you shine and set yourself apart from the masses.

When you started your yoga training, you were probably exposed to many styles of yoga and meditation, right? I'm guessing, though, that there was one thing you were immediately drawn to. After having led teacher training for years and taken a ton of them myself, I know there's always something that jumps out and makes you want to know and learn more.

Some students are drawn to more relaxing, meditative practices and others toward more fiery, active ones. This is the beauty of the yoga journey.

You want to corner the market based on your specialty. And as a teacher, whether you're a studio owner or you teach at other studios, by offering your services in a specific category, you also become premium. I learned this from one of my business coaches, Michelle Villalobos, and it made so much sense. I had been working in my niche of AcroYoga without realizing it. She brought that to light and helped me solidify my offerings so I could move forward in all my enterprises.

The difference between having a niche and not is like offering a commodity versus a premium item. Or like white bread versus heirloom-grain, batch-crafted bread. Which would you rather be: Wonder Bread for about $2 or a $25 loaf made with an ancient recipe in a small batch? You can choose either, but I want you to see the difference.

In terms of yoga, I'm not saying you need to price yourself five times higher than others, but the more you can niche yourself and create a specialty in the market—where you are the primary or one of the few who provides this service in this specific way, with obviously tons of love and attention—then you can call yourselves premium.

Let's connect this to your yoga teaching and journey.

My training was in Ashtanga Vinyasa, but two years later, I got immersed in Anusara and Iyengar, to then study Thai massage. I evolved because I kept going narrower into what I was passionate about. And even within AcroYoga, I chose to go full acrobatics, which helped me set up a ton of awesome workshops and trainings.

Finding your niche as a professional teacher might lead you to teach bigger programs or trainings, which should have your voice and your specific way of doing things. And if you've already been teaching a specific style that you're good at, then niche down as much as possible.

Your magic lies in finding your specialty. It helps you make your own recipes, your own way of doing things, and your own way of sharing this practice with the world. Knowing your magic will lead you closer to expert status. Let me guess—half the books in your library are on <insert favorite topic here>, and most of the money you spend in trainings are in this specific field? Yup, me too.

The first time I did AcroYoga, I was hooked. That was circa 2005. Shortly after, I signed up for the first teacher training and became the first AcroYoga-certified teacher in the southeast US and one of only 26 in the world!

Can you guess what that did for me? It opened every single door that I could've dreamt about to teach locally and overseas. It was my magic. I was known as Ari, the AcroYoga Queen. (I still blush when I hear that, by the way.)

Finding my magic, my niche, was a catapult to getting exposure—appearing on TV, being featured in the papers, attending performances and festivals like Wanderlust, and more.

FEEL for a moment what your magic is. What do you love to do and what are you really good at?

If you're stuck, it's okay. A lot of my clients were stuck initially too, but through some really ninja coaching, we picked their ONE thing.

You may be saying, "ONE THING?" It's okay. Take a deep breath. It will make sense soon why I'm such a big fan of niching down.

When I owned my studio, we were the only ones who taught AcroYoga in all of Miami, very niche-specific. And that gave us our claim to fame. We also offered aerial yoga and were one of the only studios in that city. So if people were searching for a specific style, it was easy to find us, because we were one of the few that offered it.

Now that doesn't mean you can't teach other modalities, but if you can pick one that makes you stand out, I suggest you go for it and go deep. This would go along with finding your population/demographic, as in where you are located. If you live in a primarily young, hip neighborhood, then you might cater to the needs of your current or future members by offering hip-hop yoga. But if you live in an older, conservative community, you will probably not make that your #1 class. (Well, maybe...older folks are pretty hip these days!)

Always think of your WHO—your ideal client—when creating offers, classes, and workshops. Also consider how you can make the students create your schedule for you. You have to be comfortable teaching something, but you want to be driven by what your audience wants.

The more you create uniqueness and are specific, the less competition you'll run into. If you call yourself a Vinyasa yoga teacher, there might be 75 other teachers or studios nearby offering the same thing. So if you can create your style, you can be more specific in terms of the outcomes you're giving. Then you are not only going to deliver a better product, it will also be easy for people to find you. You want to be findable and referable!

Even though I'm not teaching AcroYoga as much anymore, people still call me about it, because I created a name for myself. People still email the studio I owned because they knew the AcroYoga classes were there.

It's easier to market and position yourself as an expert when you're doing something you love. Because obviously you trained in something that is a little bit more specific and personal to you and your desires. Make your magic sauce and let it shine! Go deep before going wide—trust me.

put it into practice

In this activity, you will clarify your WHO, which will affect your WHAT and HOW.

1. On a piece of paper, draw a vertical line down the middle from top to bottom.

2. On the left side, write "BEFORE" and on the right, "AFTER."

3. On the left, describe your dream client *before* they work with you by asking yourself these questions.

    • Why are they coming to work with me?

    • What kinds of thoughts are holding them back?

    • How would I describe their behavior?

    • What makes them feel stuck? Why?

    • How is my service going to help them?

    • What do they desire or want most?

- What problem can I solve for them?

4. Describe your dream client *after* they work with you by asking yourself these questions.

  - How do they feel now?

  - What are they telling their friends?

  - How would I describe their behavior?

  - What kind of changes are they experiencing?

  - How much closer are they to hitting their goals?

  - How do they solve problems differently?

Meet Rosa

Rosa is one of the few highly trained therapeutic Iyengar Yoga teachers I know. She's probably one of the most experienced in south Florida. Every time I have a client with back pain, I send them to Rosa. Every time I have an ache, I go to Rosa. When I want to learn more about how to work with my clients better...I go to Rosa.

Her studio is extremely niche, so it's full of the exact type of people she can help: injured, older, stiff, those who have had hip replacements or knee operations, and people like me who simply want to learn more.

She once told me, "Ari, I am so busy with private clients—I don't need more work."

Wouldn't this be a good problem to have? I think so.

Rosa created a name for herself. She is highly recognized as a top teacher and known for Iyengar Yoga and nothing else. There is no confusion about what she does.

What If I Don't Know What I Want to Teach?

Think about this: What are you naturally inclined to do? Some teachers want to work with kids. Great, so you become a kids' yoga teacher. That's already creating a differentiation, but now we can go even further.

Ask yourself, "Do I like teaching teenagers, or do I love teaching very young children?" Working with a three-year-old is much different than working with a thirteen-year-old. So maybe you would say, "I really love working with little kids who have creative tendencies."

Perhaps you attended a specific training a few years ago that you enjoyed, and you want to do more of that. So if you don't have these specifics yet, see where you can allot your time to learn those skills so you can share them with others.

Maybe you can get an advanced certification to make you more of an expert. Think of all the ways you can help people with what you love.

Look at therapeutic yoga, for instance. You can train for more than a thousand hours and become very specific with what you know. For example, "I work with people who have scoliosis" or "I work with people who have osteoporosis."

You can't be an expert in everything; you've got to choose one or two main things to have at the forefront. That's not to say that if you're an expert at osteoporosis therapeutic yoga you can't also teach a good flow class. I guarantee we all know someone who could benefit from this type of specific treatment. (For example, I have an aunt who is 70 and showing signs of bone loss.) And once people know this, you will be referable and top of mind.

I hope all this helps you get clear about your little slice of the yoga studio pie. To get more clarity on how to find your niche, go to www.bizyogi.co/abundant for tips.

What If I Want To Teach More Than One Type Of Yoga?

If you want to teach more than one type of yoga, that's totally okay. It adds a little bit of color to your resume, repertoire, and life. But again, you can't be an expert at everything, you know?

In my area, there were more teachers of Ashtanga, but I was the only AcroYoga teacher. Did that mean I stopped teaching Ashtanga? No, because I wanted to do that and I was good at it. But AcroYoga made me "famous," brought me more recognition and money, and gave me more pleasure. It gave me a foothold in the market so I could travel and teach this very specific style without competition.

Find what you love, what you shine in. Perhaps you're an arm balance and inversion ninja. If so, do that and be the best! Niching doesn't mean you can't teach several things. You can have many styles under your belt, as there are so many beautiful practices in yoga.

As you continue your career, you might be less interested in teaching certain things. But if a private client calls one day and says, "Hey, I have your business card from two years ago, and it says you do power yoga. I'd like a private class," you can still deliver it.

Where you put your attention and focus on grows.

Keep Your Teaching Style Yours

You can keep flow in everything that you do, but you must be clear on exactly what you do and how you do it. "This is how I teach—this is my flow, this is my style, this is my authentic voice, this is what I bring to every single class!"

Even if you teach very different modalities (like Zumba at noon and Yin Yoga at 7 pm), it doesn't matter, because YOU ARE YOU and no one does what you do exactly like you. Don't lose your touch, whether you twerk to

Shakira or hold space for a transformative experience, this is the reason your clients love, follow, and trust you.

It doesn't matter where you go, students will know that if they're coming to your class, they will get exactly what they got the time before. Maybe it's a different sequence, but it's the same feel. And that's why they keep coming.

You may even have certain students follow you—they'll take your class at Studio A, they'll take your class at Studio B, and they'll take your class at Studio C. Because they love what you do, how you do it, and how it affects them.

Creating this consistent method is great for you and your marketing, and also in your pitch. If people ask you, "What do you teach?" you'll be able to explain it a little bit better. And then you create a following. You'll have your tribe of people who will want to then attend a workshop with you or take your training or go on one of your retreats. The clearer the path for people to take, the easier it is for them to follow you.

Get out there, be vocal, and don't let it slip through your hands. You've got this!

It's almost easier to create a following around yourself as a yoga teacher than as a rep for a yoga studio. People are loyal to individuals more than they are to a brand. That's why major brands hire celebrities to be their spokespeople.

Shifting Style Or Modality Without Losing Your Current Students

If a style of yoga you are teaching is no longer serving you, and it could be for emotional or mental reasons, you have the power to say—with authenticity, heart, and courage—"I'm stepping into a new place where I know I can offer more, because I've been dedicating tons of time and energy into developing this new thing that I'm bringing to the table. Thank you for being such loyal clients. I would love to have you experience this with me."

That's not always the case. Sometimes you will lose your fan base, because maybe you were teaching geriatric yoga and now you'll be teaching kids' yoga. And that's okay. Many of your students will still want to follow you because they love you. The people who don't want to follow you because they're attached more to the style are creating space for others to come in: new students, new followers. This is called evolution.

Like everything else, it takes time. You're not going to have a booming, brand-new business overnight. It's all about you stepping into that place of making the decision, maybe saying no to certain things that would prevent you from following your dream, your vision, and also creating the possibility for people to experience you in that light.

When I started teaching, I was more into a powerful style. It was more physically demanding because of my training in Ashtanga, which is a challenging practice. Then I got a little more into the therapeutic aspects of the practice. I started going a little bit softer, into a more relaxed style. But my students were used to me being more intense, which I realized because attendance started dropping.

So I asked. "Hey, I haven't seen you in class. Can you give me some honest feedback about why?"

They answered honestly, "Yeah, Ari, your classes are kind of easy now."

I was like, "Oh. Yeah, I kind of got a little softer, went a little bit more into the watery, restorative stuff."

(This is something I tell my clients all the time: Ask your students, because they know more than you do!)

A few months earlier, I had been doing stronger arm balances and inversions, but then I just got excited about this new stuff I was learning and applied it to a class without communicating the change to my students.

I realized, "Okay. So this is what they want. This is why they're coming to my class, because I've been pushing them in a stronger way to achieve some of these more physical goals." So I switched it back, and people started coming again.

When something is negative, it's an opportunity for you to step out of your comfort zone. Ask what's going on and be open to receiving real feedback, no matter what it is.

Remember this is a journey, an evolution, and a chance to discover and refine. If you find yourself frustrated or a little lost, that's okay. That's why you're reading this book and making the changes you need to lead the life you want.

Your Brand

You're stepping into yogi pro world, as I like to call it, so having a brand that's authentically you is really important. Some people will say that your brand is your smile and your message is your soul. My response to that is "Thank you, but let's get real."

As you've probably figured out by now, my style is that I don't waste time with frilly things. This book was written to get you results, and that's what I intend to do.

Always remember that "your brand is what other people say about you when you're not in the room." (Jeff Bezos, CEO of Amazon)

Start with a name. What do you want your business to be called? As a business owner, it's important that you choose whether you want the brand to be an extension of yourself, meaning in your name, or something different. There are benefits and drawbacks to both.

How do you feel about naming your business after yourself? I didn't love the idea, because I am a little bit more shy and less of a star. Also, if your business or studio is named after you, what happens if you want to sell it? On the other hand, having a business with your name might be exactly what you want and need. Think Ashtanga Yoga by Pattabhi Jois or Sean Corn Yoga.

Not naming a brand after yourself can detach it from your name so instead it becomes an entity that you create. You become the founder, the creator of this brand and maybe the specific yoga modality that comes with it. For example, if Tony Robbins wanted to sell his business and not be involved, it would be harder since his entire brand is Tony Robbins, the man.

When creating your brand, think about how you want to be represented out in the world. Connect to that bigger vision of what could happen in 10, 20, or 30 years. Also consider how the essence of a brand is so intrinsic to everything else that is attached to your business for marketing material and collateral, like your graphic design, the look and feel of your website, social media, and anything that represents your business.

If you're going to create a clothing line or other product, how can you use this brand to push it out further so you generate more revenue streams? Think about Jennifer Lopez and the empire she built based on her nickname JLo, and Jessica Alba, who created the Honest Company. Jennifer started as a dancer and now owns multimillion-dollar industries; Jessica started as an actress and changed her business to embody her values in clean products for kids. It really shows you can do anything!

Here are some parts of a brand you'll want to consider.

- Logo
- Brand Board
  - Colors
  - Graphic Elements
  - Typography
- Business Card & Flyers
- Social Media
- Website

You want to have a recognizable look that will draw attention and stay imprinted in people's minds. When a brand has that notoriety, no matter where you see it, it will recall an emotion and tie in to the value of the brand.

For example, I've been using Apple products since I was in college, and I've always relied on them for their quality and user-friendly features in addition to their aesthetics, their modern take on technology, and their future thinking. These are certain brand qualities that I'm attached to. I'm a loyal customer. When I see the Apple logo on a new product or a magazine or hear the name "Apple," I automatically get these good, yummy feelings of quality products and great service. That's what you want with your studio.

Now initially, you're probably not going to be the Apple of the yoga world, but think long term. What would happen if you franchised your studio or business and it became a worldwide name that was recognized everywhere? The brand plus the meaning and values it holds are your legacy. It's what you are putting out there, what it represents, and how people connect to it on an emotional level.

As a serial entrepreneur, I've had several companies, including my previous yoga studio, TRIO, and my business coaching programs, but none of them were named after me.

A name is something so personal that you want to take some time to choose it. Brainstorm with a friend or your coach, and feel happy when you decide on a great one!

Branding Super Start

The feeling of your image is key. You want your brand to communicate what you or your business stands for. Is it fun or serious? If you and your business are a little bit more calm, choose colors that relax people and are conducive to meditation style vibes.

Remember the brand elements listed above so you have consistency in the look and feel. How do these elements represent your vision, your heart, your ideas—those internal elements your business represents? What happens when somebody sees your website or picks up a flyer? What do they feel? "Facts tell, emotions sell." (Dave Van Hoose)

The branding, the logos, and the imagery must express your business authentically. For example, if you're a fun teacher or studio, don't make everything gray. Think of how color schemes make you feel, and how those feelings get translated and put out into the world. Create cohesive branding by sticking to your brand guidelines, giving your marketing materials the same look and feel so it's consistent. People get used to seeing your brand and knowing what kind of material you put out. This consistency helps you become a household name.

When You Can't Decide

Making decisions can sometimes be challenging, especially when it comes to the look and feel of your business. Clarity will help you find that "yes" moment and won't let you settle for something you don't like. Remember that earlier info I shared about the essence of clarity and compassionate communication?

This is when you should hire a professional such as a brand coach, a graphic designer, marketing firm, or advertising agency to support you. Communicating your idea, values, and desires for how you represent your studio with your brand takes skill. So it's critical to work with somebody who can listen to you, take in all this information, consider the emotion and the story behind it all, and take your personality into account.

If you're not sure whether you have the skills to do it on your own, do a lot of research. What other brands do you like that communicate a similar message or have integrity in the marketplace? Have a conversation with a branding professional so you can turn those ideas—those visions, that essence—into your brand. And then you'll be ready to put it out into the world.

Most Common Branding Fears and Mistakes

One common fear is that you'll be stuck with a brand you don't love. And you should truly love your brand—what it represents, what it looks like, what it feels like. Until you have that, work with whoever is the creator or the person in charge of turning your vision into those assets, until you have something you are proud of.

The #1 fear I see in branding is being complacent with something that you're not happy with. You think, "Okay, fine. This will do for now. Maybe I'll change it in the future." But that might cost you a lot of money and possibly repel your clientele. It's doable, but why not create something you love in the first place?

The second fear is the expense. Branding, when done well, is not cheap. But honestly when you're creating the face of your story, "cheap" isn't the word you want to attach to it. Quality, care, and professionalism are essential, so they come at a price. But that initial investment might be scary.

The third most common fear in branding is feeling like you don't have control, that you're not part of the conversation. You're letting somebody else create your vision, and you want to be more involved in the creation process. It depends on who you're working with, so connect with your visionary, your designer, before you get started.

As a branding coach, one thing my clients appreciate is how I just "get" them right away, even when they have no idea what they want.

One common mistake is not knowing what you want—not sharing your ideas or a vision and not being clear about your desires. If this happens, it might take a lot longer for you to establish your brand.

Keep things simple. Don't overcomplicate the process. Do the research so you can come to the table with some ideas, even samples of the look and feel you are aiming for. Maybe make a Pinterest board of your favorite companies—not only their aesthetics, but also what they represent.

Getting Help With Branding & Graphics

There are tons of different service providers who are amazing at what they do. You can browse through their portfolios to see if you like the type of work they offer.

Some of my clients don't want to let this part go. They want to do a lot of the work on their own, so their branding ends up looking wishy-washy. So maybe their websites don't match their personality, colors are inconsistent, and messages are not clear.

You can outsource by using a site like Fiverr, Upwork, FreeeUp, or 99Designs to hire people who have the talent you need for a price you can afford. Delegate to experts, and this becomes one thing don't have to worry about.

But you must have the vision and clarity to ensure you have the right connection between what you're producing and what actually lives in your heart. Remember, what you put out into the world represents you. So if what you put out isn't high-quality, doesn't have good aesthetics, isn't pleasing to the eye, it's not doing you or your brand justice.

Think about your favorite brand. What does it look like? I love Anthropologie, as it's really chic, always clean and airy, and very lux. Their merchandise is high-quality and medium- to high-priced.

Imagine somebody who doesn't know anything about you and that's the first thing they see. First impressions are everything. It takes less than seven seconds for somebody to decide whether they like you. So hiring the right person to manage and create these materials is critical.

If money is an issue, be resourceful! You can create a GoFundMe or Kickstarter campaign to raise capital. The smarter you are with your money and how you invest it, the further it can grow. Make a list of your must-haves in branding—like a logo, brand board, website, and social media templates—so that you can get your foundations covered and grow from there.

I work with my clients by empowering them to use their time and money wisely when it comes to brand and marketing creation. This makes the process easy and produces images that are professional and beautiful.

Energy Is Currency: How To Price Your Yoga Services

This subject of money pisses me off a little, because for years I considered it bad. It was the reason my parents argued sometimes, or how others in my life used it as a position of power. I almost wanted to disassociate myself from it because it caused pain in my life.

Another reason I felt this way is that I didn't value myself. So when I first opened my studio, I didn't charge enough. I thought of myself as just another teacher or just another graphic artist and didn't ask for what I was truly worth. Thankfully, that has all changed through a lot of inner work examining the roles money played in my life, the context I placed it in, and asking the hard questions. Is it true that money was the cause of my problems? Is it true that it made my parents argue? The reality is that it was not. Other factors were lack of communication and low self-worth, where money was the symbol or excuse I had chosen to put in its place.

Let's focus on money's real use. Every business runs on revenue—we all know that. The fun part is creating value-driven goodies as an exchange for that income. Your role is to set a price for what that looks like, and that's the hardest part sometimes. How do you put value on yoga? If it were up to me, I would give it away for free, and maybe you feel the same.

Here's the situation: As yoga instructors who share this practice as our livelihood, an energetic exchange of currency is healthy. We aren't the yogis of thousands of years ago. There are expenses that come with living in the modern world like eating, living, transportation, entertainment, communication, and clothing. (Unless you want to live in a loincloth like they used to!)

But setting a price for your teaching and your offerings is sometimes challenging and maybe even uncomfortable. It will differ greatly based on the location of your studio or private practice. Some metropolitan cities like New York, London, Miami, or Los Angeles might have a higher price point because of the typical lifestyle and cost of living.

Look at how things are priced throughout the marketplace. Ask yourself these questions when pricing things out:

- How much do I want to make from this (class, workshop, studio)?
- How many clients will I need to achieve that goal?
- What expenses will I have related to the location?
- What are the overhead costs for my operation?
- Who are my clients? What are their usual spending habits?
- What is the average cost of living and price conditioning of my public?

Maybe you're in a smaller town and the way of life is less expensive. For example, having a practice or studio in Manhattan is different than having one in upstate New York.

It's the same situation with your private clients. Who are your clients? For example, I had a client who is very well off and I would teach her privately on her yacht in the middle of the ocean. Teaching a private class took way more time because I had to get there, wait, teach, and then travel back home. Doing a one-hour class was really like a three-and-a-half-hour adventure! So I made sure my time was taken into consideration in the fee, as I couldn't see other clients during that time.

That client has certain standards where everything is luxury. So as an instructor, I charge luxury prices when I'm delivering luxury service. This price was fair given my 15+ years of experience teaching and my flexibility in how I served her.

The more experienced you are, the more you can charge. Think of a senior attorney at a law firm—a partner's hourly rates will be much higher than a junior's.

There is a line where honesty, experience, service, and value hold their ground and translate into higher premiums. You don't HAVE to charge premium rates just because someone is well off, but don't charge peanuts either.

When determining your pricing for services and classes, consider your clients' economic status and expectations. Are you serving this population because you know you can provide value and the cost of your time is according to what they earn? Maybe you want to help high school girls to have more self-confidence through yoga. Those prices will obviously not be as high as working with a private client on their yacht.

If you charge $150 an hour for your private yacht client, how many high school girls at $15 each would you need to make the same amount of money? ($150/$15 = 10 clients)

put it into practice

1. Consider which of your clients are high-end and which are standard.

2. Examine why that is the case and adjust as needed.

You want to feel good about what you're charging. There's a tendency for some yoga teachers to undercharge because they want to be less expensive than their competitors. They think, "If I charge less than other instructors, then of course they'll come to me." But that's not necessarily true. You don't go into a store and ask, "What's the cheapest thing I can buy?" When you want a quality product, being thrifty and smart with your money doesn't necessarily mean getting the least expensive option.

Look at the market and your clientele, and base it on your expertise. You may have a boutique studio and only offer small-group private classes. If you're providing premium services, you don't usually have the volume, so maybe three private students need to make up the amount of revenue that a class of 10 regular students would generate because of the kind of business you're creating.

If you're going on low price, then you need volume to meet your monthly goal.

Free Classes: The Real Talk

Free classes are AMAZING. Once you're clear on your desire and goal, you can decide whether some of your classes should be free or not.

For example, when you're just starting out, you could offer free classes to gain new followers. You could also do one pro bono for a charity. I'm a big fan of exchanges and trades. Perhaps you could offer a few free classes just to help people, and seeing them smile and feel good about themselves would be your payment.

Picture this: You're a studio owner who holds a special free event for International Yoga Day as a community-builder to thank your clients and members.

Or this: You're volunteering at a kids' home for an underserved population. That's a beautiful thing. It's called living from the heart and making sure that whatever you're doing doesn't take away from you living a healthy, happy life.

Always ask yourself, "Why am I doing work for free?" Is it because you don't feel like you're good enough yet? Is it because you feel like people won't want to pay you for the class because you're just starting? Look deeper into the why and consider some other options. What if you charged $5 for the class? What if you asked them to bring a donation or create a barter system?

Many people don't know what it feels like to receive and are afraid to ask. As yoga teachers, we're big givers. And that's a beautiful trait, but we also need to fill up our own cups now and again. It could be with money, a product or service, or an exchange of some sort. But energy must be circular. When you feel that abundance—when your giving comes back to you—it's lovely. I strongly believe that currency is energy and energy is currency; if there's only give, then you're depleting that resource.

Teaching for free initially is okay, but it's better to start with some sort of a trade. Also note that if you are doing work for free consistently, it lessens the value of your training. It's an energetic loop that wants to feel whole and that it's serving everyone—the students and the teacher.

How To Make Money With Yoga

As a freelance yogi, you usually make money by trading time. You teach so you get paid. You probably have one or two revenue streams like daily classes, workshops, and maybe a training. This all requires you to use your time to make your revenue.

As a coach, I think it's very important to have multiple revenue streams and feel great about how you work with them. Passive revenue and financial freedom are goals that most business owners have. (For passive income, think investments or selling products that don't require additional time.)

I like to help build passive income with my clients because it feels nice to get paid through other means. This is why I also work with dōTERRA as a wellness advocate and believe in this business model.

If you're a newer teacher, you're likely spending most of your time creating followers, clients, and loyal students. You might have a few classes a day during prime-time spots. Maybe you have a lot of moms who drop off their kids or a lot of business people who need an early-morning class. Study the demographics of your location and the behaviors of your potential clients. This applies to both studio owners creating schedules and to teachers choosing which classes they want to run.

The next thing is to test. You want time slots with the highest attendance possibilities. Remember though, these classes aren't your biggest money-makers; they're a resource for the next big thing you're creating.

Are your clients mostly parents? Start an early-morning class before the school rush and do one right after school drop-off, then see which one becomes more popular. Same thing with your evening slots—start with two evening classes at different times to make it easier for people to attend. You can always drop the one that isn't getting results.

Now it's time to get feedback from your students. The more you research, ask your client base, maybe do a poll (Survey Monkey is great for this), then make your offerings according to that.

In the first chapter, I listed different ways to make money with different business models. Let's dive a little deeper into those.

Workshops and trainings are great because they implement a model that's leveraged and can be very profitable.

Let me tell you about my client Laura. She hired me because she wasn't making the money she wanted and needed and she was traveling too much, teaching AcroYoga trainings that sometimes *cost* her money instead of making her any. We focused on one thing: Thai massage trainings in her hometown. I asked her to put blinders on and just focus on that. The result? A sold-out training with a revenue of $4,500 over two days! Sometimes being hyper-focused and releasing other things that don't serve you is the path to success.

Retreats are another great way to make money in the yoga-sphere. If you plan them correctly and balance your numbers, you could actually double your income. I've led seven-day retreats to amazing destinations and brought home five figures afterward.

Other than private clients, all other ways of making money are based on the number of people who buy your products or services.

All businesses are people-dependent, and some are leveraged and scalable. This means that serving people one-on-one limits your time, but when you offer workshops, retreats, trainings, immersions, or network marketing, you can serve many people at once. The income possibilities here are almost unlimited.

Revenue Streams Deep Dive

Let's explore the various revenue streams more closely so you can consider the pros and cons of each and determine the best ones for you and your studio.

Classes

Weekly classes are a great way to work with lots of people. They help you create your voice as a teacher, give you practice working with different people, and help you clarify the way you deliver your message.

These classes give you a platform to showcase yourself on a consistent basis. Since you have a designated time and place, you're findable and referable.

What they aren't great for is income (unless where you teach is very affluent), as the average pay for teachers ranges from $25 to $60 per class. Here's the trick, though: Establish a DEEP relationship with your students. Get them involved in your other offerings (while always respecting the studio's rules), and turn them into opportunities for higher-paying programs you create.

Workshops

Workshops are a great way to make more money and establish yourself as an expert in your field. Perhaps you've invested a lot of time into therapeutics and want to offer a three-hour session for your students.

Not only will they get a chance to learn from your experience, but imagine this...

7 students at $40 each > 7 x $40 = $280

If you split that 50/50 with the studio, you'll earn $140. But you'll also have their attention for a longer period of time, and maybe you also enroll one person in your three-month program or retreat at $1,750. This is what I am talking about. I've had workshops with 25 people at $50/per person. That was a lovely check!

One-On-One Clients

Private clients are amazing to work with as long as you charge appropriately for your time. Sell packages with bonuses or discounts, and create a great clientele who you want to work with and who want to work with you.

Trainings

The models above are your bread and butter as a yoga teacher. And you don't have to lead a 200-hour RYT; you can lead smaller trainings focusing on your specialty. You can charge from a few hundred to a few thousand dollars for your trainings. My one client Addy led her first training with 13 people for $2,950 each, or a total of $38K, which is what some people make in a year teaching weekly classes.

Retreats

Retreats are my second favorite way to change lives while making a great income. In my online course, I dive deep into the ins and outs of a retreat, as it's a double-edged sword. I know people who've lost money doing them but also know others who made five figures.

Many people think retreats need to be in a faraway land, but they could also be done closer to home. This field has tons of potential. And holding a retreat can really shift lives. Some students who came to my retreats still thank me for helping them make 180-degree shifts in their lives and practices.

Studio

A brick-and-mortar business is an amazing investment of your time and commitment. Owning a studio requires a more complex business model as you move from being a freelance teacher to a business operator. Studio ownership comes with many blessings and challenges. If this is your path, Part 2 of this book will be a great resource for you.

Online Programs

Online courses can be based on a specific topic or theme. It's one way to stop trading time for money, as you design and launch it once and then it lives on. Some of my online courses have made me $5,000 so far. They are an investment to create, but once they're done, you can resell them over and over. Challenges come in the sale and who your audience is, so it's important to have a plan for creating, marketing, and selling the course. I've helped a few clients create online programs—for anatomy trainings and breathwork—which gave them both credibility as online course creators and passive revenue.

Physical Products

You can also sell physical products at your studio such as yoga clothes, props, accessories, jewelry, essential oils, or supplements. Perhaps you see a gap in the marketplace and you create a new version of something that exists. Many companies do very well selling products. It's an initial investment but can be lucrative if you do it right. For example, check out Treelance Yoga and Funky Yoga.

Events

Every year, I coordinate The Yoga Expo of Florida. It's an amazing event that brings in over 2,500 visitors and 100 vendors and provides opportunities to more than 70 teachers. One of my clients has a smaller event called The Iyengar Yoga Conference, where she uses her niche to increase awareness of this practice.

Could you host an event as well? You might even do something smaller like a one-time event where you collaborate with other teachers, partners, or studios to give amazing experiences and get revenue streams from vendors and ticket sales.

Network Marketing

Network marketing or direct sales is often misunderstood. It takes a while to make a profit since sales are commission-based and you must spend time building a team. There are always exceptions—I know people who went from $0 to $15K in five months—but they had worked for years building an audience who loved and trusted them.

So many companies and brands align with their values and make sure they have a good pay structure. You are your own boss, so you'll reap what you put out, as with anything. I've played around with a couple of companies but have stayed with essential oils, as I align with their mission and their products. But there are so many more out there. Make sure that whoever you work with is a good mentor and leader who will train you correctly, as there's a learning curve with anything new and, at the end of the day, it's all about the sales.

put it into practice

Choose which of these models fits your passion, strengths and desire to get it out there. Having different ways of working create a broader business and help you see the opportunities for more revenue.

How Do You Pay Yourself As A Solopreneur?

One of the biggest mistakes people make when they're self-employed is not paying themselves enough (or at all), or not seeing themselves as business owners. It's so easy to keep reinvesting back in the business, right? Some solopreneurs don't even separate their business and personal income, which makes things murky and problematic. When I ask my brand coaching clients if they pay themselves a salary, most answer no.

I'm no accountant or bookkeeper, but my parents are economists and taught me to always separate business expenses from personal ones, just in case. I've had my own company for over 10 years and count every transaction under my business, which gives me tax benefits.

My parents also taught me to subdivide. Keeping your money organized and flowing gives you financial security for salaries, taxes, and business expenses. I've always worked with a simple system that is based on the way you organize your revenue, your total money coming in. You divide that revenue into at least three to five sections.

Operating Costs

First, you must understand how much it costs to run your business just to keep the doors open—to pay the bills like utilities, rent, and any help to keep the company running. Look at expenses like software, monthly and yearly subscriptions, and whatever else is vital.

Make that list now if you don't have it already.

Once you know that, look at your revenue and allocate the exact amount of money you need for operating expenses—that goes into one account or bundle. Give yourself a 5% to 10% buffer for what I call "just in case shit happens."

This is the official term in your company when you're boot-strapping things. When I had the studio, one day someone stole the copper wires to our A/C unit, which required a $2,000 repair—that's "just in case shit happens" money. Keep some in your operating expenses account so you don't have to dip into your personal or business savings accounts.

Taxes

How much money will you need to pay your accountant and the government? This is a percentage based on your revenue and will depend on where your business is registered.

Savings

You should save a small percentage (maybe 5%) to start, in a savings account that YOU DON'T TOUCH. This is money that doesn't exist until it's the end of the year and you dip into it to pay yourself a bonus or you decide what you can do with it that's fun. Woohoo!

Salary

Your salary is based on a percentage of your gross revenue, not your net. Treat your salary as an expense, or it's probably guaranteed you'll never pay yourself. Choose a percentage or perhaps a fixed amount to pay yourself monthly.

How you pay yourself will depend on your business style and where you live. For example, some people pay themselves a fixed monthly fee and some pay themselves a percentage based on sales, like a commission.

Sometimes being on payroll instead of a distribution system works in your favor. Talk to your financial professional to make the best assessment, as you want to avoid overpaying taxes or getting stuck with a lump tax sum you weren't expecting at the end of the year.

This is what it might look like:

$10,000 gross revenue

$7,000 monthly expenses and just-in-case account (rent, utilities, salaries, retail, debt)

$10,000 - $7,000 = $3,000 left over

- $1,000 goes to taxes (estimated)

- $1,000 for yourself

- $1,000 into savings

The initial account where all the revenue came in is now empty, and the subdivisions are full of their respective amounts.

put it into practice

Make your list of gross revenue, calculate your expenses, and determine your net amount.

Check out www.bizyogi.co/abundant to find a financial sheet you can play with.

With that system, you should feel like everything you're doing as the head honcho gets a return on your investment and you have a clear picture of your business.

Aiming for an end-of-year bonus feels good because you know you did great work throughout the year to make sure that all your bases were covered. Maybe you're even able to give back to a charity that's close to your heart, or donate some of that money into a scholarship fund for a student experiencing financial hardship. Think of your revenue as not only for you and your family but also for helping those who need it.

How Important Is A Business Plan?

Can I be super honest here? I didn't create my first business plan until after I closed my yoga studio. I wish I had. A business plan need not be super complicated. It's literally what it's called: a plan.

It basically structures your vision in a chart, and highlights what you might have overlooked during the excitement of opening your business. Along with a planner, this document can make those things come forth and answer questions you didn't know that you'd have.

In the book *Growing Your Business* by Mark LeBlanc, he positioned this perfectly.

I run my business:

- a) With a to-do list and no plan
- b) With a plan that contains no to-do list
- c) In my head

The most successful businesses are those with some type of written plan. Plans can come in many forms. It doesn't matter if it's short or long, simple or complex, but it makes good sense to have one.

Think of this as the Google Map of your business, important decisions, and longevity of your endeavors.

Consider some of these questions when creating your plan.

- What are your revenue streams?
- How are you delivering your services?
- What's your growth strategy?
- What are your pricing structures?
- Where are you saving for unexpected things?
- Are you distributing your finances correctly?
- Where is the money coming from?
- Do you have an investor?
- What are the loans?
- What are the interest rates?

A business plan can help out so much with these topics. Searching for business plan templates online is a great way to start sorting all this information out.

Managing My Finances For The First Time

The minute I opened my own business, I was confronted with a lot of numbers. Tracking different revenue streams and having to pay people was new for me. I had never had to pay anyone other than an accountant and some miscellaneous outsourcing.

But when you open a bigger business with others who rely on you, it's a different ball game. So a business plan helps you move forward with confidence.

For example, I learned the difference between passive and active income, and got more creative with ways to make money with less work. Before that, I believed this was only for the wealthy. One key in your business is to make as much passive income as possible from rentals, affiliate fees, and memberships.

My business plan also helped me give people opportunities to grow. I was now an empowered financial decision-maker, and that made me feel good because I was giving people jobs and money. And then, because I was learning about finances, numbers, and organization, I grew revenues by realizing which things were losing me money and which were making me money. It's easy to get lost in the day-to-day muddling and lose sight of these things, but it is very empowering once you do.

put it into practice

Keep track of these details in a journal.

How can you put energy into the things that make you money and that you love, and get rid of the things that aren't making you money or you don't enjoy?

Whether it's pricing, services, retail, or rentals, with a clear business plan, you'll be able to examine all aspects of your business and determine how they affect your financials.

This in turn will help you be more organized and create logical strategies instead of running your business based on emotions. Numbers are facts; they don't lie.

Also, make sure you have a system or software like QuickBooks or Quicken, which will help you create a routine for reviewing your numbers. And if this is something that makes you cringe, hire a good bookkeeper to handle these details for you.

We've covered so much great information in Part 1 that will give you a really clear picture of where you're at and where you can go. I am such a big fan of having these moments to sit and work on your business! You will see the differences right away in terms of your vision and how to craft a path to get there.

The next part deals with studio ownership. Even if you don't plan to own a studio, the information will be useful. For you studio owners, it has a lot of my experience plus many things I have implemented for clients that resulted in success both in their lifestyles and income.

Thank you for being part of this amazing yogic journey!

2

The Studio Owner Life

What's It Like To Own A Studio?

When I opened my studio, I had no idea what I was getting myself into. I thought it would be all peachy, because I was a great teacher and I had some business sense. But then I was like, "Oh my god, it's so much work!" FACE PLANT.

But writing this chapter brought back so many fond memories and emotions. The excitement of putting down the last piece of flooring, the day we had our first classes and welcomed so many amazing people into this sanctuary we had built. It was the biggest project of my life!

When you think about opening a studio, you must understand that you are giving the gift of yoga to others, but also that you will be the owner of a business that has many moving parts. You will need to understand all the different aspects of being a business owner and how to deal with people. This will require customer service skills, financial savvy, marketing, branding, efficient operations, effective management, and human resources skills to hire and fire people. You will have conversations that are super fulfilling to your spirit and others that might wipe you out for days. This will shift your life into decision making and require you to take bold action.

It's an experience that can be overwhelming unless you set yourself up correctly from the get-go, and it was one of my biggest learning lessons.

I had owned different businesses before, but never a brick-and-mortar one. The constant push was much more intense than I was used to. The transition from yoga teacher to studio owner required putting on a boss hat and going above and beyond to learn new things. Growth, here I come!

Some pivotal things to focus on include:

- Your mindset
- Organization skills
- Delegation
- Systems and processes

Knowing your strengths and operating within them are key. (For a list of helpful resources, check out www.bizyogi.co/abundant.)

There's a time to be humble and compassionate, and there's a time to be productive and get things done. There's a way to lead a business and be strong and be a leader so you know where to draw the line, where to create your boundaries so that the business doesn't consume you.

You want to have a lifestyle conducive to owning a business, and understand that being the face of your studio is a full-time thing. If this is your first time creating a studio or doing something like this, you must realize it does take gumption and you're in it for the long haul. It will also take a lot of being kind to yourself for making mistakes and knowing when to muscle through things that might be challenging.

There's a lot of heart and emotional stuff that goes along with it. You may open the studio as a passion project but then be confronted with situations like landlords, bills, responsibilities, irresponsible teachers, or team members that aren't pulling their weight who you have to replace. You've got to be prepared for everything.

Are You Ready?

Let's start with your studio vision. Close your eyes and envision 10 years down the road. See yourself having a successful studio and feel what that's like.

Where do you live?

What do you do every day?

How much money do you make?

In many of my goal-setting sessions with clients, they aren't sure what their business will look like in the future.

I remember doing this exercise precisely 10 years ago in my friend's living room and not having a clear idea. But then I tried it again three years later with my business coach and was so much clearer after learning about business models, revenue possibilities, and delivery methods. The befores and afters, right?

It's hard to know if you're ready to have your own studio. Maybe you've been planning it and sometimes the right opportunity presents itself to you at the right time, right place, and you just feel an easy yes coming. If it's a strong desire for you, then it's probably the right time.

Look at your vision and purpose for your life. When is the right time? When you want it to be. Here are some clues you may be ready to open your own studio.

- You've either been teaching already or you want to bring a positive asset to the community.

- You are walking down the street and see an empty space, or you have a conversation with somebody and they spark that desire in you.

- You just know you want to open a studio like I did to serve the community and have a "home."

- You want to be involved in the community in a bigger way and step into your leadership.

You will likely experience so many emotions when you open your own studio: pride, enthusiasm, fear, joy, disappointment, and all the ones in between. Owning a studio brings you to the next level of emotion and the next level of responsibility. It defines how you show up to the world.

Do a lot of market research. See what's around and ask yourself...

- Is it the right place?

- Is it the right time?

- What would happen if I failed? How would I feel about that?

If you can answer those questions and it doesn't crush your entire world, then you're in a good place.

One thing that can help you is seeing mistakes and failures as opportunities, chances to assess and improve. Jeffrey Hayzlett, a highly successful CEO, once told me, "If you're going to fail, fail fast; if you're going to win, win fast." If you can see yourself navigating these seas of failure and success without massive apprehension, then it's the right time.

Always do your homework and due diligence. Ask several studio owners a million questions. Have conversations internally and with others while you're reading this book, as all these things will give you more insight.

My main advice: Be as prepared as possible with a solid business plan, have a mentor who can help you navigate it all successfully, and do this with all your heart and soul. You got this!

Let The Love & Community In

Opening my studio was the BEST thing that ever happened to me, and I mean that. It changed my entire life from the inside out.

When you open your own studio, you will start changing people's lives immediately, starting with your students and yourself. Overcoming limiting beliefs is for sure the biggest gift that owning a business can bring you. You might employ people, thus making an impact in the local economy. You're creating a home and a community.

You will immediately have those responsibilities. While some may be drawbacks, many will also be benefits because the minute you begin you grow as a person so much. You're in charge of creating a vision, a community. You're responsible for arranging programming and managing a team, so you create a cohesive environment where they can grow and learn.

People have given countless testimonials about how much my studio changed their lives. The impact you make is much larger as an owner because you set a tone that's particular to your vision and desire, you set a value system, and you set a strong baseline for the opportunity to create a beautiful experience.

Even changing one person's life is often worth the bit of stress you may have with a vendor. Making this impact daily for dozens or hundreds of people is part of your legacy and imprint in the world.

The Struggle Is Real

As much as you will create waves of positivity and positively impact others, there are some days you will want to hide in a corner and others when you might even want to sell your business just to get out of it.

You need to be fully aware of the time investment required, which is considerable—especially at first when you're not only the visionary but also take on most of the other roles like cleaning crew, bookkeeper, teacher, manager, and front desk person.

If you thought you would have all this free time to yourself, understand that's probably not what's going to happen initially. Once a team complements your strengths (meaning they are the opposite of you), then you begin creating systems and processes that will save yourself time and energy. Procedures that can self-sustain are key.

You should budget for any financial investments needed to open the studio. Whether you are buying an existing studio or building one from scratch, you will need funds, so get ready for expenses that you foresee and allow for others that are unforeseen.

Being a boss also means dealing with unpleasant conversations. You might hire people who were your colleagues or your friends. Now that they're working for you, you will have higher expectations and they might not meet the demand.

Having those conversations as a new leader or boss might be challenging. Being a leader requires certain skills such as speaking the unspoken, being flexible yet strong when needed, and setting boundaries. For example, if a staff member is having problems and you happen to be friendly with them, some conversations might be more challenging.

Use the acronym **BRING** to look closely at issues and handle them effectively.

Boundaries: Create and respect them as much as possible with clients and team members.

Resourcefulness: Be creative with problem solving.

Intuitive: Self-care and being connected to a vision are key.

Networking: You're not alone! Tap into your yoga network for support.

Gratitude: Be grateful for the good (and bad).

Being an entrepreneur involves making sacrifices in terms of money, time, and emotions. But they are also investments. Any business you own will have the paradox of love and hate, of pouring every ounce of sweat into it and creating a lifestyle that fulfills you.

Make sure you're happy and that your vision keeps you riding the path. Enjoy all the celebrations and lessons that come into your life from these experiences.

The Studio Owner's Mindset

You may feel frustrated or overwhelmed when operating a business like a yoga studio, which has so many moving pieces. You want to think of them as challenges to overcome instead of hardships.

Let's go through some mindset issues that may arise when you are an entrepreneur.

Self-Doubt And Limiting Beliefs

"Am I good enough?"

"Am I ready for this?"

"I don't know enough."

"I don't have what it takes."

It is SO NORMAL to feel this way. And what's great is that you have yoga in your life to help you overcome it all. Learn the skills you need to move you out of doubt and into certainty. You don't need to master all the aspects of entrepreneurship, but the more you know, the more prepared you will be. I had these same challenges, but working with my business coach and doing a lot of personal development work helped me over the hurdles.

I'm All Alone

One way to prepare is to know that you're never alone. There's always somebody who knows a little bit more than you and is willing to help. Because you're in an industry where kindness and compassion are the norm, you can often tap into your network and they will lend a hand.

But being an entrepreneur is a lonely road sometimes.

Another thing you can do is to be resourceful. At a Tony Robbins talk I went to, he said, "If you don't have the resources, be resourceful." And that is a major benefit to having a business: having the bigger vision to problem solve or figure stuff out with what's around you. Sometimes you don't even need a lot of money or people. Just look to see what's around that you can connect to in order to handle each situation.

I Don't Know What I'm Doing And Am Overwhelmed

Prepare, be organized, have clarity, and connect to your why. Always make that purpose the core of all decisions you make. Keep fresh in your mind why you opened your studio. Why did you choose and create this lifestyle and business model for yourself? How will that benefit others? Rely on your team to take care of things you can't, and take it day by day.

Always connect to that, because the roads might change a little bit, but the core will always be the same. So if you're firmly grounded in the why—the bigger reason—and to your vision for what you're creating, then many of the things that might come in as challenges or hardships become learning opportunities or experiences, or your biggest teachers. Listen to your heart, then make that connection between heart and mind, knowing you're not alone and that the more resourceful you are, the easier it will be to overcome any obstacles.

Confront things as they come with a clear mind and a deep breath. As you know, breath is super important in everything we do because it calms us. And know that there's always a solution. As Marie Forleo, a prominent business coach, says, "Everything is figureoutable."

When Shit Hits The Fan

There will definitely be a moment—or many of them—when shit happens. So it's best to be prepared for the unexpected (as much as you can be).

A couple of examples come to mind from my own studio that seemed awful at the time but now make me laugh. One time, we had a huge event with 40+ people. All of a sudden, water started coming out of the bathroom into the yoga room. The A/C had broken, so water was falling from the ceiling and flooding the bathroom. Another time, the police called to say that someone had stolen all the copper wires from the entire building, so we had no power for a day or two.

These were small shits. A bigger shit was arguing with the landlord over an unexpected $4,500 bill.

When you feel overwhelmed and stressed out, try to stay connected to your grander vision. Have a goal and that larger why. Don't operate on problem solving day-to-day stuff. Work *on* your business and *in* your business so you won't have as many in the first place.

Sometimes dealing with relationships and managing a team and your business might be challenging, but know there is always a way to step into your role as leader and balance things out. It's okay if things don't always work perfectly, because this is where you learn the most!

Trust and seek support when hard times come your way. And guess what? It's also okay to let go of some things, recover, and then receive the lesson or gift.

One aspect of leadership (apart from choosing your wall color, writing checks, and making a schedule) is the communication with your staff members, who are integral to its growth and success. Having a communication style that helps you to speak the unspoken, create dynamic relationships, and serve both you and your staff is key.

The Logistics Of Studio Ownership

Let's move on from mindset and emotion into some tangible pieces of being a business owner that help in opening and creating the business.

Here's what you'll learn about:

- Brand & Name
- Business Partners
- Consistency
- Hiring A Staff
- Location
- Marketing
- Networking
- Operations

Branding And Naming Your Studio

When you're naming your business and creating your brand, you want it to be unique. How many yoga businesses are named the same? Try to be different and stand out. This doesn't mean you should pick a complicated name, but go deeper and connect to it emotionally.

Explore the opportunities to name your business a word in your native language. There are only so many Sanskrit words that can be used without the name being too difficult to remember or spell. Name it something with meaning to you that is also attractive to your audience and easy to find and write. You want a name that's easy to remember and spell.

By the way, you can always change it in the future, as long as that change doesn't cost you thousands of dollars and all your work to build the brand (because that's not easy or cheap). The easier it is to find and connect with, the more likely clients will come to your studio.

There are tons of ways you can name your studio, such as...

- City you're in (EX: Weston Yoga)
- A word you connect with (EX: Yoga Tree)
- Something fun (EX: Green Monkey)
- Sanskrit term (EX: Aum Yoga)
- Strong words (EX: Core Power Yoga)

My favorite is to find something you connect with.

Is it a good idea to name your studio after the city it's in? Maybe. But you don't want to pigeonhole yourself with that name so you always have to be in that city. If you are thinking of growth, create something you can change without it affecting the studio name. For example, Miami Yoga Studio could limit the brand to Miami. But if you have no desire to have more than one studio, then it doesn't matter. It might actually work in your favor in terms of SEO and marketing.

There's a successful studio called The Yoga Joint, and they add the name of the city to differentiate the location. CorePower Yoga has multiple locations, and they just list the city names on their site and marketing.

This applies to your website as well, so take your time in naming the studio. Brainstorm, ask students and friends who you trust, research the web—and who knows, you might get divine inspiration for the name!

There are so many great things to remember about when we opened our studio. There were three owners, so the studio name was TRIO. It was authentic because yoga unites the mind, body, and spirit. It was that triumvirate of the three aspects and three owners. It was special that we came up with that name, and we were glad it wasn't already taken.

Now I'll tell you the mega-crappy, annoying, and time-consuming thing that occurred. Soon after we opened, we received a cease and desist letter from Tri Yoga stating we could not use the name Trio Yoga as it was a copyright violation. (Insert panic attack here.) I had already designed our logo and branding and had spent $1,300 on the sign outside the door. We had to act quick, consulted a lawyer, and changed it to TRIO Studios, as that was not in violation of the copyright.

So please check copyrights. Google the Trademark Electronic Search System, or TESS, and do some digging for trademarks™, copyrights ©, and registered names®. Don't get stuck like we did. Like I said before, do your research before you step into anything big like branding.

Finding Your Location

Having a prime location can be important to your business, especially when you're just beginning. Location can mean you have foot traffic or maybe it's visible from the road. These things could make the cost much higher as well though.

Here are some things to consider.

- Is it in a residential area or a more commercial area? This might affect your schedule and your marketing.

- Is it easy to get to? The easier it is to reach, the more students you will have and probably retain.

- Is there ample parking? If the studio is in a "driving city" like mine was in Miami, parking was a must.

- Do people already congregate there? This makes community building and being seen easier.

- Is it close to other studios? If it is, you might want to make sure you are unique and create your authentic offering. But competition is healthy, by the way.

- Who lives nearby? Knowing your ideal clientele helps you create offerings and market in a way that appeals to their specific needs and interests.

You want to make it convenient for people to get to your studio. If you've already built a big following—you have a good size email list and solid social media presence—you could open a studio on a second floor, and your rent automatically becomes a little bit lower. Or if you don't have many students yet and you want to save money on rent, you might be able to pump it into marketing dollars.

If you want to keep your costs low, you can go to a less popular spot. I know tons of people who opened their studios on a first floor and, after growing their clientele, found a more affordable location nearby. It's okay to stop paying for a storefront location if you no longer need it.

In many studios, having a high rent creates financial hardships initially. But once you have an existing clientele and you have tons of members and you have a nice store and people are buying stuff, it gets A LOT easier.

Shopping Center Vs. Stand-Alone Building

I've seen studios thrive in all different kinds of shopping centers. There could be a closed-in shopping center like a mall or maybe more of an open-air shopping center where you have access to more foot traffic. If there are other businesses with a similar vibe nearby, it can enhance the visibility of your studio.

Where you are located doesn't always guarantee success; the quality of how you serve your public and the amount of "noise" you make in marketing and visibility will be what makes you successful.

More and more, I see yoga studios opening in non-streetfront locations, warehouses, or the back or second floor of buildings, because there's usually a discount on the rent. The operating expenses are smaller, and they can probably still market enough to have a good influx of students.

There are both benefits and drawbacks to having a stand-alone building. Are you the only building within a five-mile radius, or are you close enough to other businesses that they're helping through visibility and accessibility? If you're in a mall in some obscure corner where no one can see you, that might be a drawback because you're still paying premium rates for a storefront, yet you don't have the visibility that other businesses would bring.

Also, look at the other businesses around you. Are there any with your target demographic? Perhaps you're in a shopping mall. You have this high-powered yoga and fun classes geared to 20- to 40-year-olds, but the businesses around you are more for 60- to 70-year-olds. You must ask yourself if the businesses around you will have a demographic that would help you.

But it would be very advantageous if you're in a shopping mall accentuating self-care with cool stores and service providers or a spa nearby. See what's around you and determine if that's going to serve your venture or not. Your location should be strategic enough that it's easy for people to come to.

Buying Your Own Building

Buying instead of renting is a great option if you have the money, and it is an investment for the future.

One of my clients who has a thriving studio in her hometown did exactly this. She bought the building where her studio is as a lifelong investment and now owns an asset that goes beyond the studio as a business, also cutting down her monthly expenses.

Just make sure you go down your list of the WHYs for owning your own building. Here are some I suggest:

- The investment won't put your finances in jeopardy.
- The area is growing with more businesses.
- It's an asset.
- Your return on investment will be worth it.

One piece of advice in any venture you undergo: Do some research and then do more. There were times when being naïve cost us not only time but also emotional distress and a ton of money.

The landlord's goal is to rent out the space. And with a commercial space, the rules are a bit different than for a residential one.

Make sure that your lease agreement is reviewed by a commercial real estate lawyer who keeps your best interests in mind. Read the lease carefully and make sure the terms are acceptable for both parties and you're protected for things like repairs and lease increases.

Your current landlord may be the nicest person, but what if they sell the building to someone who is not so nice? Pay special attention to details on property repairs, extra costs, taxes, fees, and rent increases. All those little things you might not think are important might become so at some point.

For example, there might be a plumbing issue and you have to pay a $3,000 bill. But maybe by changing one or two words or adding a clause to the contract, that would've been the landlord's responsibility instead of yours.

Think in terms of longevity and make sure there are options to renew and to protect yourself as a tenant.

Finally, maintain a professional relationship with your landlord, even if they are your friend.

How Do I Keep My Current Students If I Move?

The cool thing about teaching at a yoga studio is that there's a sense of loyalty and deeper connection with your students. Yoga is not just a physical, fun workout; it delves deep into spiritual, mental, and emotional places and facilitates relationship building.

The good news is that if you're providing a good experience and you move to a new spot that's still convenient for the students, most of them will follow you to your new location.

PRO TIP: Offer an incentive like: "For everybody that comes to the new location, we're offering a bonus class!" or "We're going to do X, Y, and Z for our loyal clients." Maybe it's free parking if they usually have to pay, or the first class is free. Give them something so they feel welcomed into the new space.

Once you impact someone's life, they will want to stay connected.

Changing locations will also likely bring a bunch of new people to your business. And it will be fun to welcome a whole new tribe.

To Partner Or Not To Partner, That Is The Question

I've had business partners and I've also operated solo. They both have their pros and cons. If you decide to have a partnership, you can distribute the workload, and you might do things together so it doesn't feel as scary. If you complement each other, have great conversations, and tend to agree on most things, then maybe they can handle some things you don't enjoy but they're good at.

It's comforting to have somebody to lean on who cares about the business as much as you do, because you both put the time and money into it. Someone to share the good days and empathize with you on bad days. If you have complementary styles, the relationship can grow your business a lot more. You have two people fighting for the success of one business versus one person having that entire weight on their shoulders and maybe not having the resources, whether it's financial or the know-how, to create a team to do what that second person would do.

There's a HUGE difference between hiring someone to work for you and having a partner. As a business owner, you are the visionary and the one who will delegate to others in order to reach that vision, knowing fully that your employees will often put in much less effort than you do. Why? Because it's not THEIR business (aka their "baby").

Make sure you have clarity around who's doing what, who is putting more time in, how much your time is worth, and what you're bringing to the table other than money or disputes might arise.

Let's say your studio cost $50K to build and both of you put in $25K—then you're starting at an equal level. But what if one person puts in a little bit more? How are you bringing yourselves back to a 50/50 partnership? (Note that this is different from an investor who gives you the capital, which you pay back with interest.)

Every situation will be a little different, but you CAN do it on your own supported by a team. Imagine two or three years into the future when your studio is successful and making good money. You get to keep all that money instead of having to split it.

Consider what kind of a partner you want. Two people with very similar work styles who are good at the same things might actually be counterproductive. For example, if both of you are creative but aren't very task-oriented, how are things going to get done? Build a partnership that's complementary, like cogs in a clock, where everyone plays their part to keep the system running.

Think about the different phases of a partnership: pre-business, in business, and afterward—the exit strategy.

With two (or more) leaders, uncomfortable conversations and disagreements will arise around money, time invested, stress, legal issues, and big decisions, which might not be the most pleasant convos. So considering all these things initially will save you a lot of time, work, and possible headaches, and also is more likely to result in a beautiful relationship.

Know yourself—the way you work, the way you want things done—and realize that your partner has their own way. Be clear, truthful, open, receptive, bold, courageous, and wise...and your heart and mind will guide you to answer whether or not you want a partner.

On the other hand, not having a partner allows you to operate solo and be completely in charge of YOUR business. You make all the decisions and bear the weight of being the owner, but in my opinion and experience it's more satisfying. Also, my business coach, Michelle Villalobos, told me once that close to 90% of partnerships don't work out.

Being the sole owner allows you to hire a team that supports your vision. You also get to keep all the profits. I've coached both people in partnerships and those who operate solo, and ultimately the more successful ones have been on their own.

Who Should Be The Face Of The Company?

Do you want your face on marketing material and your name all over social media? Or does the thought of that make your skin crawl? It can be scary stuff putting yourself out there. As a business owner, you might want to be the star of the show or you might not, and either one is okay.

Someone who is personable and outgoing should be the face of the company versus someone very shy who doesn't feel as comfortable facing the public.

Your brand need not be you; it can be your creation. For example, Oprah IS her brand. It's her face everywhere you go. On the other hand, the shapewear SPANX was created by Sarah Blakely, but if she sells the brand tomorrow, it will affect nothing.

When deciding which partner should be the face of your company, this mantra I wrote comes in handy:

> We speak the unspoken. We both step up into leadership and come to agreements that serve both. We serve the highest purpose of truth, honesty, communication, and love. We decide based on the greater good that serves us, the community, and spirit. We act with self-love and respect versus selfishness and ego.

What happens when there's poor communication? When you don't speak the unspoken because you are scared or because the other person has an overpowering personality?

Discord. You might both agree that it should be neither of you, and instead just use a stock image, because that way you both have equal play. Perhaps you do a photo shoot and both of you appear on the website. It depends on your mutual desires, individual strengths, and clarity—communication that comes from empowered, authentic deep understanding of what you want as an owner and sharing that vision with your partner.

How To Split Finances Between Partners

Regarding the financial split between partners, there must always be clear agreement, which can stem from how the partnership began. If it began with an equal monetary contribution from both parties, you should create a partnership agreement to reflect that equality.

Or perhaps you contributed money equally but agreed that one partner would take the lead role, whether it was running the studio or teaching classes. In that case, you'll need to mutually decide what the percentage split is.

If there's an investor, you must also factor that into your agreement. Having an investor is not exactly like having a partner, but you must still factor in fair compensation when splitting up the finances.

Always look at your expenses.

- What are your day-to-day expenses?
- What are your monthly expenses?
- What are your miscellaneous or unexpected expenses?

From that total revenue, deduct your operating expense to determine your surplus.

put it into practice

1. Make a list of your current or expected costs

2. Create a scenario of ideal revenue. This will also help you plan to achieve your target revenues.

3. Now do the math. Does this number make you feel abundant? Is it enough to sustain you?

Numbers don't lie and it's a good practice to maintain for your monthly or quarterly projections and goals as well as seeing what you want to do to reach and surpass them.

Now that you've figured out your surplus (or profits), you must decide how you will manage it. Are you going to pay yourself through your agreed-upon split? Are you going to reinvest some of that money into the business and then split what's left?

If you've already calculated marketing and repair costs, and you are dividing the "buckets" to cover these areas, there is no need to reinvest in the business because you're already covering everything it needs. So you can just split the money as agreed.

I suggest you get all your agreements, contracts, and important assets on paper. You might even have a mediator, a financial advisor, or a lawyer review it. And consider having someone organize your money, such as a bookkeeper or an accountant, who can look at everything from an outsider's viewpoint. Protecting yourself and your business is important to make sure you have your vision in alignment with laws, taxes, and others. The more organized you are, the clearer outcomes will be.

Dividing Up The Work Between Partners

When dividing up work tasks, the desire is balance, but the reality is that sometimes things just need to get done.

put it into practice

Make a list of all the tasks that need to happen in the following key areas to have a smoothly running business.

- Customer Support

- Finance

- Human Resources

- Legal

- Marketing

- Operations

- Sales

- Technology

Then I suggest you go by strengths—what brings you the most joy and what you are good at. Because once you identify that, you can look at the other tasks. This gives you the opportunity to look at the ones you're not so good at so you can delegate, maybe have an expert come in and take over.

I'm not the best at numbers. I love them—I love to see the influx, I can write checks and balance books. But I'm not good at keeping budgets and things like that. And when I owned my studio, who was the finance person? Me. So I not only hated doing it, but I also took twice as long because I kept pushing it off. Not a win-win. My solution: I hired a bookkeeper. Because they love numbers and are good at their trade. This saved me time and money. Problem solved.

Hire others to support you so you can focus on what you love to do and are good at.

My Experience In Partnership

In my original business with a partner, there wasn't a lot of clarity initially. We ran the business on survival mode without taking the time to focus on our vision or our individual strengths and desires. This is why I am such an advocate for clarity.

Think of a time when you've had this issue in other parts of your life, perhaps with a friend or a loved one, and how it affected the relationship. A business can intensify this because there are money and livelihoods involved.

Despite these problems, there was also a lot of fun and lightheartedness in my business. Dividing up and delegating between us was also a time to be proud of our qualities and skills. My partner was a great networker. She was active and had great relationships with people.

There are some things that nobody wants to do, like spending three hours at the city office to get permits. Sometimes you take one for the team. So we'd take turns doing the fun and pleasant tasks and the tedious ones. If one of us sat at the city office for hours, the other would do another time-consuming task. Like I mentioned earlier, balance was the goal.

We created a harmonious environment, and this is why we had one of the best studios in Miami. It was one of the greatest experiences of my life and taught me so much about teamwork, collaboration, and leadership.

When Your Partner Isn't Pulling Their Weight

This is one of the tough conversations I'm referring to. When you have to give honest constructive feedback, people tend to get emotional. It all goes back to your initial partnership agreement. It doesn't just say: "You own this percentage of this business and I own this percentage of this business." It also details expectations, job titles, and tasks for each person.

You might be gifted with numbers and your partner might be a marketing wizard. As the numbers person, you'll know if marketing isn't bringing in any students, and that's a conversation you'll need to have. If your partner gets a check for the wrong amount, that's also a conversation. So depending on what is happening, always go back to that partnership agreement and the responsibility you took on as an owner.

One fact that I learned years ago from my business coach is that most partnerships don't work. Fortunately, there's a beautiful piece inside the agreement called an exit clause.

What happens if...

...you're no longer happy running this business?

...you decide you want to do something else with your life?

...you don't want to be a yoga teacher anymore?

...you move and can no longer run the business from where you are?

The answer? You have an exit strategy. You might sell your part of the business, buy out your partner, or even bring in a third party. So that agreement covers what happens in case of "what if."

Always speak your truth, from the "I" viewpoint and with an open heart, while also being firm about your desires. Create a win-win scenario as often as possible for the health of this amazing relationship you've chosen to be in.

A good friend of mine who's a professional mediator helped me shift my communication in this way and it made all the difference. When confronting someone, a partner or even an employee, say something like "This is what I am looking for" instead of pointing the finger and saying, "You didn't do this right." This makes for an empowered conversation instead of one where you are simply blaming and showing others their mistakes.

Communication With Your Yoga Studio Team

In moments when you must speak the unspoken, meaning you say the hard and difficult things, you put yourself in a vulnerable position. But instead of seeing vulnerability as weakness, consider it an opportunity for growth.

Owning a business requires a huge investment of time, money, and resources. And sometimes speaking the hard truths, not only with others but also with yourself, is powerfully liberating.

This might mean having a sit-down with an employee, a business partner, or yourself and having to say things that make your stomach turn. It might mean firing someone or quitting. Truth (*satya*) is the baseline for life, and keeping things inside does not reflect that.

COACH TIP: Practice conversations with a mentor or coach before you have them with your employee. My biggest lesson was speaking from the "I" perspective (owning my truth and power) versus the "you" perspective (blame and guilt).

Never take things personally. Go back to the partnership agreement and make that a baseline for your relationship with yourself and others.

Remember, we all come with emotions and past experiences, so be kind yet firm in how you speak.

This is all third- and fourth-chakra stuff. I practice third-chakra RAM and fourth-chakra HAM mantras to balance out energies before I have a difficult conversation. You can access these mantras online www.bizyogi.co/abundant. They help you connect to a deeper power and change your energetic state.

Running The Business And Hiring Staff

How many hours should I expect to spend running my own business? This is a question my clients ask me often.

Are you part of the bootstrapping club? Oh you don't know about it? It's a club for all people starting businesses who have relatively little income and are either doing most things themselves or have just enough money to hire a little help.

Initially, if you don't have an assistant, a manager, or cleaning staff, then expect to work a lot of hours. There's always something to do—something to organize, some sort of marketing, administrative tasks, or a customer or potential customer waiting to hear from you.

If you own a studio, plan on wearing 17 different hats, from janitor to bookkeeper to lead teacher. Until you have a staff in place, expect to put a lot of your time and effort into the studio by physically being there and getting stuff done. But as your revenues grow and you allocate some funds for the extra help, you'll spend less and less time doing things you don't enjoy. Then you'll mostly be dedicating your heart, soul, and time to ensuring that your business succeeds, so you'll be happy and making plenty of money.

As you start delegating, you'll realize, "I would like a life. I need time to spend with my family, to spend with myself." Usually, self-care is the first thing we give up, but it's so vital for running our businesses. I mean consider what can go wrong when you let go of taking care of yourself and your priorities outside of studio and business life. Pretty much all the not-yogi things you can think of. Your health might take a toll, you might be overwhelmed and stressed, miss out on social activities, see your kids less...just pile it on.

COACH TIP: Outsourcing is one of the best ways to free up your time. Check out www.bizyogi.co/abundant for resources on outsourcing.

When To Expand Your Schedule With More Teachers

Growing a studio and a following requires having a staff to expand the schedule. From the beginning, look for teachers with the same values as you, who maybe have a complementary vibe and might be able to attract a different crowd like a different age group or more of a certain sex. Your employees should also embrace your studio's philosophy and brand.

Create a small team of teachers who will be an asset to grow your studio through their quality, their way of showing up, their marketing, and their strengths as teachers and yogi entrepreneurs.

Interview and hire right away, even if it's just one more person to help balance things out. Your students will demand variety, because having the same teacher all the time can get a little boring.

Asking For Help...FREEDOM!

If you don't have it already, getting help is the magical unicorn that will help you get your time and life back on track.

First, assess where the gaps are, the things you love and hate to do. Initially, you will probably do everything on your own because you might not have the funds or hiring savvy, or might not need someone right away.

If you can't handle a project on your own, at least get temporary help to get you started and get the ball rolling. If you are wise with your time and dollars, you can cover a lot of bases without going broke or saying, "I can't afford this."

One of the biggest mistakes is trying to do everything on your own, then doing it half-assed so it turns into a huge cleanup project. Whoever takes on that task will have to redo half the stuff you tried to do, which usually costs you twice as much.

As you begin to get more movement, incoming traffic, and revenue, you can delegate that money to the right people, the right projects, and the right tasks. Most likely you will still handle certain daily tasks and operating procedures, because you know your business better than anybody else.

To do this effectively, you need to have a solid idea about where to put your spending to create more ease in your day-to-day operations. Whether it's a manager, a front desk staff, or support systems like software to automate certain tasks or run the backend of your studio, you'll gain time and freedom.

Moolah Time! Paying Your People

Aside from your rent, payroll will be your largest expense. You want to be fair to your teachers without going broke. Be smart about how you pay so that it's mutually beneficial. My mom, who has a double masters in economy and is a genius (Love you, Mom!), said payroll is the most crucial expense to have sorted from the beginning. It can always shift, but it's one thing you must have thought out carefully so you come in with a plan.

Here are some scenarios that illustrate how you can pay your teachers.

- Flat Rate Method: No matter how many people show up, whether it's 1 person or 30, you pay your teachers the same amount. If your studio is full, this turns out to be the most economic, but if you're just starting out, this might be a large expense.

- Variable: You start with a base, so let's say from 0 to 5 students they get $20, and for every person who attends after that, they get an additional $2 to $3. Some studios offer a no-show rate and then move upwards from there, as well as having a maximum amount they can make so your payroll doesn't fly through the roof.

- Per Student: You pay purely per student. So let's say each attendee earns them $5, $6, or $7, depending on how you want to pay your teachers, how much you can afford, and what the standard is. So if they have 30 people, they're getting paid $6 per person and walk out with $180.

- Percentage: You pay them a percentage of the total revenue. So you might give them 30% of the total amount that their class made. This one gets tricky and could be more problematic than beneficial. It can be hard to track since studios run on different packages, social deals, and specials.

In my opinion, the Variable Method is the most mutually beneficial way to go for both the studio and the teachers. The base rate determines how much more you pay. For example, if your base rate is low, you might want to give a little bit more per person on top; if your base rate is higher, you might pay a little less per extra person.

Also, if your studio has a high volume, do you eventually cap the pay? Let's say you're giving a $25 base and then $2 per head on every student after the fifth one, but you have a 30-student class. So now you have 25 people x $2 = $50. Add in the base rate of $25 and that's a $75 class.

put it into practice

1. Detail some likely scenarios at your studio.

2. Do the math to make sure what you're offering is sustainable.

Now, you don't want to be known as a studio that doesn't pay well either. So find a balance between how much money you can allocate toward payroll and how much is a decent amount for a teacher.

You also want to motivate your teachers to increase their attendance and marketing to bring more people to their classes. If you see that a particular teacher is doing a great job, you can offer them special bonuses, awards, or gifts to incentivize them to keep being awesome. This is lucrative for both you and your teachers.

Getting Your Studio Out There

Marketing: Communicating Your Brand's Message Effectively

Marketing is vital for any business to increase sales and revenue. You want to constantly put your studio or yourself out there for the public to see, for people to experience, in order to grow your business. And because you're reading this, it's likely that you're looking advice on this topic.

It's the principle of business growth where you promote your services, products, and brand to create a fan base of yogis who want to practice at your studio.

In my case, it was always a question of "How can we give more value to our students?" In our emails, we asked for their opinions by conducting polls each month and giving a breakdown of the results. We got away from doing the usual "come join us" or "here's our special" kind of emails. Every email became an opportunity for people to learn a little bit more about yoga, to get a different tip, or to meet one of our instructors. So it wasn't about selling services; it was about creating relationships.

As a result, more people replied to our emails—which they weren't doing before—so our engagement grew. They commented, "Oh thank you so much for that! I never knew about that particular pose." They became more interested and were eager to see the next newsletter. Our email open rates went up quite a bit, which was great.

Our membership went up as well. Our students became more loyal because they saw that the studio wasn't just about selling workshops or more memberships, it was about establishing a culture of valuable yoga practices. They understood that we were serious. That's why we grew to be one of the top yoga studios in Miami several years in a row. (And that was a huge honor because Miami is enormous, with many yoga studios to choose from.)

It's crucial that you're always out there spreading the goodness of your classes and services. The more you expose and promote your business, deliver your authentic message, and rock out your services, the more customers you will gain.

Marketing Fundamentals

First, as you've learned, creating an effective vision, mission, brand, and website are major building blocks of your marketing campaign. Have a website that's content-rich and easy to navigate. The minute a customer lands on your homepage, you want them to be able to access information easily so they can learn about what you do and how you do it while getting value.

Value is the baseline of all good marketing.

Second, how do you attract these people? Imagine a funnel—you want to invite your future customers to enter your world. The process of how they move through this world to become a loyal client is their journey. A fundamental part of getting a customer to the next stage of the journey is having a clear goal of the action you want them to take. This is another reason your website and landing page must be organized well with the information easily and readily available.

Also, figure out where these clients are coming from by doing market research and identifying the types of clientele you want.

There are two types of marketing: inbound and outbound. An example of inbound marketing is when someone uses a search engine like Google or Yahoo and finds you. For this to be a viable source of clientele, you should have smart search-engine optimization. For example, if someone's searching for "yoga Manhattan," your studio should come up on the results page. This is usually based upon a keyword search of your website, which is why sites that have content rich with keywords will come up higher in the ranking or in search engines. This is something you can talk to your web designer about.

An example of outbound marketing would be paying for ads on Google Ads, Facebook, Instagram, YouTube, LinkedIn, or wherever your ideal clients will be most likely to find you. Paid ad strategies require specific knowledge, so I suggest you speak to an expert. Many of these sites have people you can talk to and get you started correctly. You don't want to pay for ads without a strategy and baseline knowledge.

YouTube is one of the largest search engines. Having a YouTube presence will help attract people to what you do and create interest in learning more about you by going to your website or clicking on a special offer you have. You can start a channel with yoga videos to promote your style, philosophy, and vibe and be connected to a new audience.

The clearer you are about the action you want the customer to take, the more your effort makes sense. You need organization, structure, and systems. For example, if you're doing the marketing yourself and your focus is to have five new clients this month, you would create an offer and spend $X on social media ads. Because you know your clients hang out on Instagram a lot, you post an ad there and target it to people within a five-mile radius of your studio, including a picture or video to drive curiosity. Then review the results and adjust as needed. Always split test to learn what works and what doesn't.

Types Of Marketing For Your Business

Once your branding is taken care of, you're ready to really get the marketing machine up and running!

All business owners want the same thing: prosperity in all aspects of their business and life. How they get there is with more clients doing yoga, falling in love with the practice, and becoming your biggest fans. What does this do? It creates loyalty, steady income streams, and a life that gives you ultimate freedom. The fastest way to get there is through intelligent and effective marketing.

The bottom line is getting new clients and retaining your existing ones. You make your business the shiny path to feeling good, looking good, and ultimately being good. This creates a cycle where you're constantly getting new clients, changing their lives, and keeping them involved with greater offerings like retreats, trainings, and practices to take them to the next level.

What do you do for new clients?

There is an art to crafting a great offer that not only incentivizes them to show up but also to stay. For example, as a teacher, you can work with the studio to use their promotions as incentives. Or if you're looking for new one-on-one clients or people to join your programs, you might want to offer a special introductory price or a bonus incentive.

I've seen a ton of "first class free" promos or "$7 for 7 days," but those doesn't always do the job. When people don't invest money initially, there's less chance of them spending more. I did a test with a free class vs. a two-for-one offer and we had more retention and initial income with the latter.

Maybe you can do an introductory offer that encourages the clients to take a few classes and get to know the feel of the studio. This will be something very personal. You know your audience. You know how your studio works and how you pay your teachers. Regardless of what you offer as an incentive, make sure you feel good about it. Some examples include a two-for-one, intro special at 50% off, special new member monthly membership price, or a bundle where you offer a bonus if they get a specific deal.

Here's what this looks like.

1. You place an ad on social media, where your potential clients learn about your studio.

2. The client visits your studio and you WOW them with stellar teachers and amazing facilities. (Even if you're small, you can create an impact.) Find creative ways to make them feel special.

3. Use your conversion (sales) process to turn them into membership clients, because as we all know that's the ultimate goal.

Your ad should be something that's going to motivate them to come and check out your studio, especially if there's a lot of competition. How do you create that curiosity and get them excited about coming to try your studio versus the one down the street or in the next town?

In marketing, the word "curiosity" is key. Nowadays, we're so bombarded with offers and sales, specials, "Buy this," and "Come here," you need to really stand out. So in your ad, make people extra curious about why they should click on the offer or your website. If they're checking you out on a print ad, you need to make them pick up the phone and call. Nurture each customer and make them feel like they belong and they are the most important person in your eyes.

Having a sales system will be a key component in your operating procedures. As technology progresses, it's best to focus on digital marketing to get your message out because it's so versatile and easily accessible. This format also allows people to interact with your marketing.

Regardless of your method, testing your marketing in terms of product, price or promotion, and place are key.

put it into practice

Answer each question below to get more clarity on your customers' "YES" to your offer.

- Product: What am I offering and why is it attractive to a new client? Why would they want to spend money on my studio's offerings?

- Price or Promotion: Is the price point of the promo I'm offering attractive to my potential client? Why or why not?

- Place: List the platforms I will put my ad on (social media or online). Which ones serve me best based on my demographic?

Offering Value As A Marketing Tactic

In digital marketing, there are ways you can show off your business and brand as having exceptional quality by giving people a taste of what you know and offer. This is a tactic called lead generation through content-based marketing.

Check out some great ways you can provide value.

- A guide on how to get the most out of your yoga class

- Great recipes for the season

- A description of your favorite practice

- A video tour of your studio

- A chapter from your most recent e-book

- A Top 10 guide of yoga poses for stress

- Your best tips for a safe yoga practice

- Audio mediation and guide

The list goes on. It can be really fun to brainstorm creative ideas that will help current and potential clients get a feel for your studio and your style.

As you know, yoga is a practice. It's something the students do to create a shift in their being. So when they come into your studio for a discounted or free class, they have an experience, they get a vibe. And there are so many cool ways to deliver that yoga experience as a little pre-frame that encourages them to check you out.

At the end of the day, however you can capture your people's attention puts you one step closer to creating a relationship with them where they become part of your family at the studio, loyal students, and raving fans.

Offline Marketing Strategies

Offline marketing is another excellent way to create relationships with possible clients. Consider having a joint venture, which means creating a partnership with another local business. I have always loved this, as you can give each other's business value. Perhaps they offer a coupon for your studio and you promote them on your website. We did events and yoga classes in healthy restaurants that exposed us to a totally new audience and made their clients happy.

Another way is to attend events where you have a booth or a table that's branded, where people can get information. You could give in-person offers and easily track where the response is coming from, if you're working with different venues, with either special coupon codes or email lists.

Start networking by going to different venues where you can meet people and create that kind of relationship. Also, you could be a featured speaker and be in a position where you're giving information, perhaps about the wellness benefits of yoga and meditation in the lives of busy people. You can do these events for corporate clients or for bigger organizations. Just make sure that your ideal clients will be there.

You don't go to these events "just because." You go because you're hoping to grow the audience at your studio. And there are also big benefits to having a wider audience, because perhaps you get booked to teach in other places, which creates an additional revenue stream for you and your studio.

Get out there and make yourself visible! Share what you offer, how you offer it, and why it's important for others to experience. This can be accomplished much more easily in person as you can get direct feedback. This is your chance to leave a lasting impression, because people can look in your eyes and shake your hand, and you can leave them wanting more.

What comes next? Promote and sell event specials, pass out your fliers, connect with them on a personal level, take their information, and then send them follow-up emails. There're so many different ways to create these partnerships and to be present at networking events where you can share the best side of you and your studio.

My Biggest Marketing Fails

My #1 biggest mistake was not marketing enough, specifically not spending money on Facebook ads. We feared spending money and did not feel savvy enough at the time to know the ins and outs. Chances are that had we implemented more Facebook ads and produced more online YouTube content, we would've had more students and increased revenues. It wasn't a big monetary loss, but it hampered our growth.

Since every "failure" is an opportunity to learn, improve, and redo, it was always a learning experience when we didn't reach our revenue goal, where we asked ourselves why that had happened and what we could've done better.

Even when what you're doing is working, there's always room for growth, because technology and marketing tactics change so quickly. See marketing as not just how you are selling your products and services, but also as one possible way to uplift a person's life. Then it's almost your duty to market and to offer services in an authentic way.

Marketing is simply a strategy for putting your stuff out there—your services, your studio, your brand, whatever you're wanting to grow. Everything you do is an opportunity for growth and showcasing your vision, mission, and message.

Does your brand have a consciousness aspect? Does it create an environment of health and wellness and constantly allow that to be the baseline, the foundation? Understanding and implementing that will be one of the most tangible ways to see your studio and practice grow. Seeing that bigger change in your students as more revenue comes into your life means the more you can serve, the more attention you can place on your students, and the better services you can provide.

At the end of the day, the more effective your marketing is, the more income your studio makes and the more sustainable and successful business you create. This affects your life and the lives of your employees as well as your community.

put it into practice

1. Make a list of all the amazing things that having more revenue could do for you and others.

2. Close your eyes and visualize it and write it all down.

3. Create your ideal scenario with the money your business made and see how this can even affect your legacy in the world.

Marketing Advice
For Biz Yogis

Don't do it all yourself. Use the limited time you have in the most efficient way possible.

If you don't know marketing, you have two options:

1. Spend time learning how to market. Use your resources wisely, create very specific and targeted ads, monitor your results, and adjust as needed.

2. Hire a specialist to do it for you so you can focus on what you do best. This investment will come back to you in leads.

Use a good service provider to get staff—somebody who cares and is invested in your growth. Don't hire a person who isn't going to give you what you want and need for your business. Do your research, ask around, and make sure they specialize in what you need.

- Do they specialize in small business growth?

- Can they market your events?

- Can they help you grow your following?

- Are they familiar with and successful at marketing other businesses like yours?

If you're marketing by yourself, know what you're doing so you don't waste money and time. You might make your money back, but you can't get your time back. Before deciding to do it yourself, just know that you will need to invest in time and learning. You will get what you pay for, so don't be cheap with your investments.

Marketing is such a specific trade that even though I had a career in the marketing and branding sphere, I still had people help me. I didn't want to invest $200 on a Facebook ad that produced zero results because I didn't set up my reach correctly or I didn't use the right picture or effective copy.

Imagine hiring somebody to help you and getting five new clients from the ads they run. That new income will pay for the Facebook ad and for their time.

I'd rather pay extra money and get back double my investment. Be smart with your resources, be honest about what you can do given your capacity, or leverage what somebody else can do to bring you new clients.

Marketing Time Wasters

One of the biggest time wasters in marketing is not having a clear strategy or knowing what you're doing. Facebook and Instagram ads can be very tricky to set up. Just throwing stuff out there without results is a time waster.

Boosting posts to the world for example is pretty easy, right? But for better results, instead of hitting the boost button, take a few extra minutes to dedicate ad spend and target the right audience.

I like to say, "Spending money on ads without a strategy is like peeing in the wind."

WOW Your Students!

As part of your marketing efforts, you should strive to wow your clients by giving them special treatment when they've spent money on you. To get inspired, go online and search for promotional products.

Some ideas include:

- Branded apparel
- Goody bag with several items
- Magnets
- Mugs
- Notebooks
- Totes
- Water bottles
- Yoga towels

For higher-paying clients, who perhaps purchased a VIP package or your top-tiered offering special, consider giving even more valuable thank-you gifts. Not only will they feel appreciated, the item you give will remind them of you and your studio every time they see it—bonus marketing!

Another way you can market yourself is by wearing branded gear. Whether it be yoga shirts or hats, make sure you and your staff have your studio's swag on when teaching and when out at events. Mega bonus if the apparel is also wearable for daily use. There's no such thing as too much brand exposure!

What kind of message should be on the item? Maybe it's a positive saying that inspires your students to get to class more often, or something funny. Match your brand's feel to what you put out, so it reminds people of you. There needs to be congruence among your brand, your studio, and your promotional products.

Make your swag and branded promo material something that represents you and your brand and connects with your pillars of WHY you have your business and how these items support that vision. Avoid items that don't align and stay with healthy, organic, and sustainable products.

Remember, you can also ask your students what they would like to receive with a quick survey. Services like Google Forms, JotForm, and SurveyMonkey can help you collect the responses.

The Social Media Web: Digital Networking

Think of social media as a massive online form of networking. The best part is not having to drive anywhere, while still being able to meet cool people. There are tons of online groups besides Facebook, such as blogs, forums, and meetups. As with all marketing, a good social media campaign requires a lot of strategy, so focus on the goals you want to achieve, then make your task list.

Social media is a huge way to reach an audience. It gives you a broader local reach and can take your brand worldwide, literally. The key players (as of 2020 when I'm writing this) are Instagram, Facebook, LinkedIn, Twitter, and YouTube. But of course, this is subject to change over time as new platforms arise and others become obsolete.

The best way to interact on social media is to give value, especially with a Facebook Group. Maybe people are asking questions you can answer, or you can give feedback and get noticed. Giving value and having conversations is a perfect way to network online.

When I read people's comments, sometimes I click on their profile and send a personal message to get to know them. This is how you get noticed more—attraction and connection marketing at its finest.

Be wary of wasting time on social media though. Have a focused outcome, and only participate in groups that have your ideal audience for your business growth goals.

If your business is location-dependent, there are tons of local digital groups where you can learn a lot about what people want to help grow your business.

Participate anywhere you can be seen, give value or advice, or share your thoughts. This can spark bigger conversations that lead to someone's interest in trying your studio or class.

Interaction can also lead to sales, so be tactful in how you connect with people. You must sound genuinely interested in their well-being instead of selling in such a way that's off-putting. Have the mindset of "Let's get to know each other." Ask questions and get to know them so that when you meet them in person, there will be an instant rapport. Get to know what they like and what they don't like.

Social media helps to cultivate interaction, and that's what humans are all about. It's creating relationships and opportunities for us to connect and thrive.

Below are some tips for a few social media platforms.

Facebook

- Stay in touch by sharing updates on life.
- Post photos that showcase your studio, community, and vibe.
- Connect with friends and followers.
- Create a group so you can effectively interact and have a social experience online.

Instagram/Instagram Stories

- Record brief videos as reality TV through the use of Stories and lives.

- Use IG Stories to tell people what's happening in your business at that moment.

- Curate some of your best moments on the feed.

YouTube

- Create a channel for your brand.

- Use it as a vlog (video log).

- Create awesome how-to videos that teach and show your expertise.

- Build a following of people who want to learn more about you.

- Reach an audience of people searching for exactly what you're putting out there.

Video Marketing

Nowadays, people prefer to receive information visually, so video is one of the top ways to introduce your audience to who you are and have them get to know you. A good welcome video can take you from a complete unknown to a welcomed visitor in just a few minutes.

Video is a great way for you to show your personality because people can look you in the eye. This is more effective than when they visit your website, which has great information but no real personal connection.

Take the time to create a video that will show off your vibe and your energy and provide a ton of information in a short amount of time. For example, think of when you're texting somebody. It can take twice as long to get your message across as it would when you speak on the phone or FaceTime.

More and more, platforms like YouTube, Instagram TV, and Facebook Live are becoming great ways to promote our yoga studios, health, and wellness, and to keep the growth of this beautiful trend alive.

How Often Should You Put Out Fresh Video Content?

To create steady and digestible content via video, do what is sustainable so you can be consistent. Ask yourself how often you want to film, and have a dedicated film day for best results.

Before shooting your video, decide what you're trying to say and how you want to accomplish it. Ask yourself, "What is my purpose for doing this?" Decide what action you want them to take, and then work backward. For example, if your goal is to invite people to a special class, you can either do a few videos that are a little bit longer than normal or a lot that are brief. It depends on your personality and the attention span of your ideal audience. When deciding what kind of video to create, consider what attracts your current students most.

Some great ways that video can boost your engagement and connection to your digital audience include:

- Announce new products, classes or sales you might be having.
- Tell people about a workshop, training, or retreats.
- Introduce your staff members.
- Hold mini-trainings that can help people in their yoga, meditation, or breathing practices.
- Explain your studio culture. People love to see behind the scenes.
- Give sneak peaks of live events to encourage some FOMO (fear of missing out) for those who didn't participate.
- Show off your signature style, if your studio has one. Perhaps use how-to videos that get people excited about working with you and your staff.

It's helpful to understand the basics of video, such as having good lighting and sound. If you're speaking, make sure people can hear you clearly. Invest in a good microphone—it doesn't need to be expensive, but it should be high-quality. While you're recording, look past the camera and speak to your audience. After the video is recorded, you will need to edit and publish it.

Use this checklist when recording videos.

1. Decide what action you want viewers to take at the end of the video.

2. Use the Who, Why, What, Now formula.

3. Write out and practice what you will say before recording.

4. Determine the primary purpose of the video.

5. Aim for the ideal video length. If it's content-heavy, the video should be longer; otherwise, make it short and sweet. Remember, people want to be engaged in the content but not overwhelmed or, even worse, bored.

6. Record your video with visual clarity using proper lighting and a decent camera. These days, you can even get great recordings on a cell phone.

7. Adjust the audio so it's recorded clearly and you can be heard above any background noise.

8. Pick a day and time to regularly post your video content, and be consistent.

Inconsistency will hurt your video marketing efforts, but not doing it at all is worse. If people know you usually put out content on a certain day at a certain time, they will be expecting your notifications. Think of people wanting to watch their favorite yogi online at the same time and in the same place.

Whatever you choose should be appropriate for the end result you have in mind. Focus on the styles of classes at your studio, give some value-based how-to tutorials or yoga classes, or give lectures on wellness or nutrition aligned to your brand.

For an extra income stream that will take your brand nationwide or worldwide, do an online yoga class. You can create several videos or "sessions" so that for a monthly subscription, people can take your yoga classes in the convenience of their own homes and whenever they have the time.

The more that people can get to know what you do, how you do it, and why you do it, the more your studio will grow. Create videos on a YouTube channel, on your Facebook page, or on your website to support those three pillars.

There are so many ways of using video to your advantage, but the key to creating effective video content is to always keep your goal in mind. Make it fun, make it personable, make it you!

Growing Your Yoga Biz

Since the yoga world is so much about community and building your tribe, being out there in front of people showing your face and sharing your energy is super important. At small events or large, through networking, you can always find somebody to connect with one-on-one, somebody to guide in a more positive direction.

First, find where your people are. Do a little research. Perhaps your neighborhood or local businesses have groups you can visit. Find a good place where you feel comfortable sharing information.

The more you can give, the more you can chime in and offer suggestions. That's where people will see you, hear about your business, and then ask questions to learn even more. It's all about initiating the conversation. From there, a lot of beautiful things can happen.

It might lead to collaboration with an owner of a similar business so you can cocreate and grow together. Maybe it's a student who's interested in going to your retreats and partnering with you in another profitable venture.

How To Network Effectively

No matter where you live, you can find events related to health and wellness. Participate at these events as a speaker, or have a booth representing your studio. For example, my event The Yoga Expo is a great place for studio teachers and owners to show off their teaching style, brand, and products. Check festivals and other expo-like events for a booth, a teaching spot, or a simple connection.

Sometimes you go to events just to learn, listen, and meet other people. The main thing is to go with a clear purpose and intention. Once you do that, every person you meet will be a gateway to a new client or a different opportunity to grow the business.

Think of where your ideal audience is. Spend your time participating in events that benefit you and them so it's a win-win. You get to meet a bunch of possible new clients, they get to be exposed to your awesomeness, and the wealth of yoga is passed on further!

For example, if your practice caters to an older population of professional women, go to networking events where these types of students might be. You can pass out your cards and fliers or offer free classes for people to try. Maybe you give a goody or hold a raffle. Anything you can do to stand out and connect with more people.

There's a quote in sales by Zig Ziglar (What a name, huh?) that says, "Success is not a destination, it's a journey." Connecting to a new and broader audience is part of that journey.

Again, be clear about your purpose for going to an event. If it's to be in partnership with somebody to help grow your business through their network or their audience, find out where those kinds of businesses are. Maybe it's a Chamber of Commerce, or more specifically, the Holistic Chamber of Commerce in your area.

Be smart with your time and energy so you really get the most out of your participation.

When Networking Is Not Your Thing

You might be thinking, "Ari, I don't like networking" or "I've had kind of crappy experiences in the past."

Can I be brutally honest here? I didn't like networking either. I tend to freeze and feel like a wallflower most of the time, so I can definitely share some bad experiences. I am naturally shy. I stay closer to the walls versus going up to people and introducing myself and shaking hands and commanding attention. But I have learned to adjust my behavior because it wasn't serving me. I've learned to ease into networking and be more authentic in how I connect, so I don't feel weird or uncomfortable.

So ask yourself whether you are the best person to represent your business at networking events. I'm definitely NOT the ideal person to be thrown into a crowd of people I don't know.

At one of the largest networking events I went to, my coach Michelle grabbed me by the hand and pulled me into the middle of the room with her. She just dragged me along because she's very outgoing. She was introducing herself to everyone, saying "Hi" and asking people's names, while I was living my worst nightmare. I was mortified. But someone like my husband, Marcel, is a great person for networking because he could make friends with a rock!

So What's The Solution?

After that event, my friend and coach got a few prospects and at least one or two new clients for her business. She asked me, "Ari, do you think coming to this event and staying by the wall serves you or your possible customers?"

I said, "No, it doesn't. It actually takes away from me being able to share what I love, which I know would be really beneficial for everybody."

If you're going to networking events and you are a wallflower, that may not be the best use of your time. But maybe you can have a friend come with you who's more outgoing. Or have a representative go as an ambassador for your studio or business, if you know that will be more beneficial.

If you haven't had much luck participating in events, it might be you weren't prepared with your pitch, maybe you didn't bring business cards, or you just weren't feeling inspired. Just know that it's okay.

put it into practice

1. Take a moment to reflect on your strengths and ask yourself if you are going to be the networking person for your business.

2. Next, look for some optimal opportunities to attend when you can connect with your ideal audience, and mark those on your calendar.

3. Prepare before the event to make it super rewarding. At the event, pass out your cards, collect names and emails so that you can add them to your email list, and invite them to experience your space and classes.

4. If you need more ideas or are stuck, talk to your business coach. "This is what I've been doing, but it's not working. What can I do better?" Observe, assess, and then improve.

Community Events

Being highly involved in your local community, supporting businesses in your area that are complementary to yours, and joining activities can be amazing ways to get your name out there.

Besides networking, it's important to be involved in community, sports, or charitable events. Volunteer your time, and show that you're not just about having people come to the studio to spend money. It's about you being a leader in the community and giving back. You're leading and living from a place of what yoga really is. It's also a great way to make friends with community leaders or people in local government.

Make sure that you're not just going to networking events to get clients, but also to be part of the community and give back. Just because you're running a business doesn't mean that your yogic principles are to be thrown out the window.

Align yourself according to your values.

It's not about being everywhere all the time. That's why we have marketing, that's why we have ambassadors. Choose how you can participate to the fullest. Like I said, maybe you become a sponsor of an event and play a bigger part. It's better than having a small part at several. How can you benefit most, both in giving and receiving?

Now that you know where to go and what to do when you get there, make sure you have a follow-up strategy like sending out a personalized email, connecting on social media, making a phone call, or sending a text to stay connected. Know that the more you put into new relationships, the more you'll get out. This helps create more systems and processes to increase both your student base and your revenues.

Taking Care Of Your Clients

Do you remember the TV show *Cheers*? The bar's theme was "Where everybody knows your name." This is the energy you want in your business.

You want people to grow accustomed to a pattern where they understand your ideas, your energy, your flow, and your classes so they know what to expect.

Be consistent and add your flair, your magical way of doing things. What if you become the master of adventure and surprise within a framework that works for you?

There's a great book called by Michael Gerber *The E-Myth Revisited*. He talks about when he went into a barber shop, and the first day they gave him a nice warm cup of tea. The next time, he only got a glass of water, and the third time he get nothing. What happened to the barber shop? You can probably guess that it had a decline of repeat customers. Once people are used to exceptional service, they'll be upset once it's gone. So give your people tea every time or not at all!

Think about it—if you're teaching and every time you use aromatherapy or maybe you give a little massage after class, people expect that they will get that yummy treat and it might even be the main reason they go.

Because you've set this precedent where your clients and students are used to excellence, they might be disappointed if it suddenly goes away.

Perhaps every time a customer purchases a class pass or signs up for a workshop, they get a little something extra in their bag. Or when they join as a member, they get a goody bag. Maybe you have free cucumber water available during classes. What would happen if suddenly you stopped doing that? People would wonder what changed. (And you know people don't like change.)

When you take things away, you'll likely have upset customers. I can't count the number of times where I've been that grumpy customer and been turned off because something wasn't the same anymore, or there was a new employee who didn't provide the same level of service I was used to.

If you're doing something consistently—the way you show up to your class, your energy, your teaching—and then you add something to wow your students, that will add value. But then you need to be consistent. Your students will come to count on it and may even brag about it to their friends.

Don't stop wowing your current and potential students. Don't diminish the quality you're providing. Because a dip in quality will eventually lead to a dip in your revenue.

Being Consistent As An Owner

Here's where systems and processes come in so handy to help you create consistency in the business world. Remember, you want normal people doing exceptional things. And let's face it—no one will ever do something as well as you. The best piece of advice I got from a customer was, "You'll be lucky if your employees give 70% of the energy you would give...and 70% is asking for a lot."

Why do I mention this? Because if you give 110% and turn that into a system (think checklists, training videos, levels of expectation), you have a better chance of someone coming in and being able to efficiently manage or run the studio, so you can dedicate your attention elsewhere.

You want to have systems and processes in place that help your business run smoothly and are consistent as well as manageable so you and your team never feel overwhelmed.

Students, who are the main reason we want to have an amazing studio, have different and sometimes more rigid expectations than ourselves.

- Cleanliness of the studio from the props, the mats, bathrooms, floors, and welcome area.

- Organization schedule, updates, class changes, and how you run your business. This even applies to how their accounts are handled.

- Punctuality of when classes begin and end. This is important if your teachers open the studio for their classes. Arriving five minutes late to find students waiting at your front door is not acceptable.

- Pricing your classes and offerings correctly so that perceived value is received well by your audience. This might include social deals as well.

- Personal touch so that there's a special feeling being transmitted.

These are nonnegotiables for running your studio and must be consistent in-house. But think of the WOW factor. What can you add to create constant relationship growth?

As a studio owner, you should set a high standard from the beginning and maintain it using these systems and processes to create a level of quality where you always meet or exceed your clients' expectations. It's creating an established norm that your clients love and are used to, and having organization among your staff. Make sure that the system and procedures are set up and run correctly, so consistency is maintained no matter who is using them. These could include...

- Opening and closing duty checklists for teachers and front desk staff

- Instructions on how to answer the phone and reply to emails

- Procedures for handling common customer service scenarios

- Emergency procedures

The moment we implemented systems and processes like these, our studio's energy flowed much more fluidly and there was also less micromanaging. We freed up time as owners and managers.

put it into practice

1. Make a list of operating systems that would help your business feel more coherent and smooth.

2. Map out the process or checklist for each.

3. Share these with your staff.

4. Keep a binder or online folder with all these systems for easy reference.

5. Update or supplement them as needed, maybe quarterly.

Every aspect of your business, including marketing and branding, should be consistent. That way, you're always in front of people showing the best version of you and your studio, and you're always running the business efficiently. You create habits for your staff and for your students as well.

How can you use your resources and strengths to create high levels of quality that translate into stellar customer service?

Whether it's the style of class, the atmosphere in your studio, the teachers, or the retail products you sell, there should be unity between what you are putting out there and your client's experience of what you've built.

From the beginning, your messaging is the most important. Whether it's a Facebook Ad, an Instagram post, or a Pinterest board, it should be a positive representation of your services, of what people will receive when they sign up to work with you or join your studio.

Also, be consistent with your operations in-house—both front-of-house with your students and back-of-house with your instructors. Having high-quality operational standards will create loyalty from your customer base and also among those who work for you.

Your employees and brand ambassador should be a great representation of your company's values and an instant preview of what it's like coming to your studio.

When you choose ambassadors, position yourself as a speaker, or attend networking events, it's even more important to ensure everything is aligned. How your ambassadors act, communicate, and relate to people are a direct representation of you, your studio, and the values you hold.

How you run your business, especially for yogis, should always be authentic in terms of your voice and your message. Promising things you can't deliver or failing to effectively represent your services are both disconnecting from this authenticity.

Organizational Tips To Support Business Operations

As I mentioned, I'm big fan of technology. I believe it's best to organize anything you can such as front desk manuals, operating procedures, and branding elements. Many online services are cloud-based so you can store information and access it easily.

Some great tools I use are...

- Asana
- Dropbox

- Evernote
- Google Drive
- Trello

All of these will be your BFFs. For example, Evernote, Trello, and Asana are all project management software that can help you keep track of the events, ideas, and projects for your studio. Google Drive and Dropbox are cloud-based storage solutions where you can keep your files neat and organized and accessible from anywhere.

If you don't love technology or have a hard time using these tools, you can seek help from a virtual assistant. This can free up your time to handle other tasks.

Creating Consistency With A Brand-New Studio

If you're a brand-new studio, all you want to focus on right now are sales, marketing, and customer service. Then little by little, you'll create your processes and systems. But first, you must have paid students to implement them.

When I first opened my studio, we didn't have a lot of clarity. We just wanted to open the doors, get people in, and excite them using whatever resources we had. Over time, our brand—the images we used and our messaging—changed a little bit. But because we were delivering such high-quality service, nobody cared. Our loyal students were there from day one until the day we closed. To this day, people still ask us about the studio.

Connect to the idea that nothing in life is permanent except for change. And if you deliver exceptional service, that change might just be a blink in time. So relax, breathe, and smile!

Focus on sales and marketing. Make sure you have longevity. Then make smart investments into reworking your brand or redesigning your website.

The more you focus on getting people in the door and wowing them, the more success and growth you will experience. YOU GOT THIS!

Conclusion: You Have A Yoga Studio...Now What?

After doing all this work—the branding, the sales, the marketing...all the things—what do you do now?

The moment you allow yourself to think bigger and see further, you know there's a bigger reason and you astound yourself with the limitless potential. You move out of being a yoga teacher to a business owner, and you have a larger platform to make a difference on a larger scale.

Remember to celebrate. Honor yourself and your journey.

Allow time for things to settle, and ask for help when you need it.

Check in with yourself every so often to see whether you're happy and your cup is full. Don't be afraid to reassess often, and let go of anything that adds stress and anxiety to open up for new and fresh energy to flow.

I could have written 100 more pages in this book, as the journey of being an entrepreneur is endless and has its ups and downs. I have tried surfing many times, and it's always scary, fun, and thrilling all at once. Owning a business is similar—ride the wave.

What's cool is that from here on out, you can focus on scaling your business, creating financial freedom for yourself through more revenue streams, or maybe chucking it all and traveling the world. It's all in your hands and how you make your destiny.

Step into your flow, your breath, and your grace, as that is the path to success. It's not about the money; it's about your happiness, health, and wealth. Let the abundant yogi in you step into your greatness and ask for what you want in life and from life.

Stay connected to your inner truth without sacrificing yourself.

Know that I love you and that the Universe supports and believes in you.

Thank you for being on this yogi journey with me, and please stay connected so we can keep sharing and growing together!

Acknowledgements

I honor all the teachers in my life who taught me what yoga is, beyond just asanas.

MEGA thanks to my parents, Juan and Isabel, for creating me and making sure I did "my" thing my entire life without trying to stop my independent and adventurous ways.

To my husband, Marcel, for being my rock and my eternal sunshine (and my massage therapist when I was typing all day).

To my daughter who was born the day after I finished this book... thanks for waiting!

To my fur babies, who watched and wondered, *When are we going for our walk?*

I am eternally grateful to all my teachers and all my students, who made me a better teacher through their support, and to my friends who understand me in all my peculiarities and love me for that.

Big thanks to Diana and Amy for reading this book and helping me edit and to Julie Willson, who helped me revise and shape this book into a second "baby" with her editorial feedback.

Most of all, I'm grateful to yoga for changing my life upside-down and right-side up.

References

Chopra, Deepak. ChopraCenter.com.

Dunn, Brennan. "Should You Niche Yourself?" DoubleYourFreelancing. com. https://www.doubleyourfreelancing.com/Niche/.

Gerber, Michael. *The E-Myth Revisited: Why Most Small Businesses Don't Work and What To Do About It.* Harper Business, 2004.

Gibbons, Serenity. "You And Your Business Have 7 Seconds To Make A First Impression: Here's How To Succeed" Forbes.com. June 19, 2018. https://www.forbes.com/sites/serenitygibbons/2018/06/19/you-have-7-seconds-to-make-a-first-impression-heres-how-to-succeed/#172894ac56c2.

Guru Mantra. JivamuktiYoga.com. March 2009. https://jivamuktiyoga.com/fotm/guru-mantra/.

LeBlanc, Mark. Growing Your Business! Expert Publishing, Inc., 2003.

Michalowicz, Mike. *Profit First: Transform Your Business From a Cash-Eating Monster to a Money-Making Machine.* Portfolio, 2017 (reissue).

Sinek, Simon. *Start With Why: How Great Leaders Inspire Everyone To Take Action.* Portfolio, 2009.

About The Author

Arianne is the creator of Biz Yogi, an international yoga teacher and thought leader, owner of the Yoga Expo Florida, and a lover of life, travel, and all things health, wealth, and happiness! She brings 15+ years of experience to her students, whether they be yoga practitioners or yoga teachers looking for their next phase in business.

A wildly passionate entrepreneur, Ari infuses her love for yoga and business to bring your heart and soul into your life. Nothing is more exciting to her than finding passion and being free to travel and work anywhere.

Biz Yogi is an online platform with a course and coaching for creative gypsy souls like you to maximize your expertise and passion and your business so that you can create more light in the world, because as you know, all change starts with your decision to act.

People know Ari as a mover and a quick-thinking, solution-based yogini. She's constantly inspired to make work feel fun through her light-hearted approach, silliness, effort, passion, and dedication. Given her experience in the yoga industry building programs, trainings, retreats, and the Yoga Expo, you are in for a treat!

Arianne "Om" Traverso was born in Peru and moved to Miami, Florida, to be around people of all different cultures and backgrounds. After graduating cum laude with a BFA in graphic design, she became a yogi, strapped on her travel shoes, and explored the world. She became the first AcroYoga teacher in the southeastern United States and is currently one of the top 10 teachers in the country.

Ari has spent more than a decade in the yoga industry building programs, trainings, and retreats and managing a successful studio in Miami. She now focuses on helping others achieve similar success at Biz Yogi, a socially conscious company that gives a percent of its profits to local and international charities. Ari enjoys spending time with her husband and baby daughter.